A guide to The Wealdway

John H.N. Mason

A guide to
The Wealdway

Constable London

First published in Great Britain 1984
by Constable and Company Ltd
10 Orange Street London WC2H 7EG
Copyright © 1984 John H.N. Mason
ISBN 0 09 464820 4
Set in Times New Roman 9pt by
Inforum Ltd Portsmouth
Printed and bound in Great Britain
by The Pitman Press Bath

Contents

Illustrations

The maps were drawn by Baxter & Brand M/MSIAD.
The photographs were taken by Tom Sawyer.

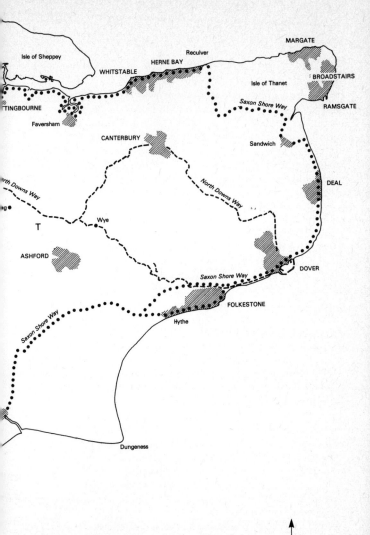

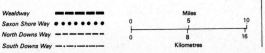

	Miles	
0	5	10
0	8	16
	Kilometres	

Wealdway ▬▬▬▬▬
Saxon Shore Way ●●●●●●●
North Downs Way ─ ─ ─ ─ ─
South Downs Way ─·─·─·─·─

Isle of Sheppey
SITTINGBOURNE
Faversham
WHITSTABLE
HERNE BAY
Reculver
MARGATE
BROADSTAIRS
RAMSGATE
Isle of Thanet
Saxon Shore Way
Sandwich
DEAL
CANTERBURY
North Downs Way
North Downs Way
Wye
DOVER
ASHFORD
Saxon Shore Way
FOLKESTONE
Hythe
Saxon Shore Way
Dungeness

Introduction

In introducing this guide to the Wealdway I would first of all like to pay tribute to those who conceived the idea of a long-distance route for walkers from the Thames to the English Channel across the Weald. The Wealdway is a country route of 80 miles from Gravesend to Eastbourne, formed for the greater part of its length by linking existing rights-of-way. It was originally the conception of the Ramblers' Association in 1970 but motorway building and other factors held matters up and the first definitive guide *Wealdway* was published by the Wealdway Steering Group in 1981 with a separate supplement (re-issued in 1982) for accommodation and transport details.

One aspect of the Steering Group's achievement is that by promoting the Wealdway a comparatively little-known area has been opened up for walkers. Although perhaps without the spectacular attractions of the better-known North and South Downs the Weald is full of beauty and interest. The chief attraction is its variety: on parts of the Wealdway you can walk for miles without seeing a human habitation or along the rich meadows by the side of the Medway. The bare upland heath of Ashdown Forest contrasts with the dense oak and beech of Five Hundred Acre Wood on its borders. There are ancient churches, old inns and timbered manor houses – a real treasure chest, with stretches of the North and South Downs at either end for good measure!

In common with the other Constable pictorial guides the aim of this volume is not only to help you find the right path but also to act as a travelling companion by supplementing the directions with a running commentary on the country passed through: its history; its present features; the significance of particular aspects: anything that is likely to enhance the enjoyment of the walker and to stimulate interest in the many facets of this most pleasant part of the south-east.

In the guide the Wealdway has been divided into eight sections. The format is the same for each section:

General description

This is a summary of the main features of the section: the going, the
gradients, the type of country passed through and any particular
items of historic or other interest. At the end of each general
description are given the numbers of the Ordnance Survey 1:50 000
and 1:25 000 series maps that cover that section of the Wealdway.
In the latest Pathfinder series of the os 1:25 000 maps of the area
the Wealdway is specially marked – another tribute to the
Wealdway Steering Group.

Route

Detailed directions for finding the correct route are given *in both
directions*: firstly, for 'southbound' walkers, i.e. those walking the
Wealdway in the direction from Gravesend to Eastbourne, and
secondly, for 'northbound' walkers in the Eastbourne–Gravesend
direction.

In the text for the 'southbound' walkers will also be found
descriptive material on the country, villages passed through and
other features considered to be of interest. Useful information, for
example whether there is a pub and what time the Post Office Stores
are open, is also given.

The descriptive material is not repeated in the text for
'northbound' walkers, but the features for which such descriptions
exist are shown with an asterisk, denoting that these are to be found
in the 'southbound' text.

Suggested diversions

In some of the sections of the guide there are suggested diversions.
These cover places of outstanding attraction – examples are
Cobham, Penshurst and Alfriston – that are only a mile or two from
the Wealdway route. Although such villages may be on the tourist
circuit they each have features of rare interest: the nineteen brasses
of Cobham church, the Hall of Penshurst Place and the
fourteenth-century Clergy House at Alfriston, for example, and I
have felt that the Wealdway walker might be disappointed if he or
she had not been told of them and how they could be reached.

Detailed directions and sketch maps are given on how to reach the places concerned from the Wealdway, using footpaths as much as possible, both for 'southbound' and 'northbound' walkers.

Public transport and accommodation
At the end of each section there are details of public transport facilities and addresses of suitable, reasonably priced bed and breakfast accommodation *en route*. Many of these addresses are taken from the Ramblers' Association *Bed and Breakfast Guide* and as such are often based on recommendations from members. For anyone who enjoys walking in Britain this accommodation guide, published annually, is a great boon.

Public transport
Information on rail and bus services is based on time-tables in operation at the time of writing and is liable to change. It is vital therefore to check timings, etc. well beforehand. Current time-tables are sometimes to be found in bus shelters and at bus-stops but you cannot rely on this. Public libraries *en route* usually have a stock of time-table leaflets for bus services in their area as do village Post Offices or stores. The telephone numbers of the service enquiry offices of the Maidstone & District and the Southdown Bus Companies are given in the text.

Accommodation
The establishments shown in this guide should be able to offer comfortable accommodation and good food and are accustomed to cater for walkers. Such arrangements are however as liable to change as is everything else.

The Wealdway
The word 'waymark' has been frequently used in this guide and probably needs explanation. The local authorities in England and Wales have a responsibility to see that all public rights-of-way in the country, i.e. public footpaths and public bridle-paths, are indicated by signposts at points where they start or finish at a metalled highway or where they cross a metalled highway. The signposts can be of the 'tall post' type with a 'fingerpost' showing the direction of

the path, or a low concrete post marked 'Public Footpath' or 'Public Bridle-way'. Unfortunately owing to vandalism or sometimes lack of funds to carry out the necessary work many signposts are missing; the low concrete posts have the disadvantage of occasionally being invisible because they are covered by roadside vegetation such as long grass or brambles.

In addition to the official signposts 'waymarks' are used, generally at intermediate points along a right-of-way where there may be difficulty or doubt. These waymarks are usually arrows painted or fixed on stiles, gate posts or sometimes trees to show the correct route. They can also be used, as for the Wealdway, to distinguish an officially recognised long-distance path. You will therefore find the special waymark of the Wealdway, the WW sign, at all points of vantage along the route. Unlike signposts, the fixing of waymarks is optional but each needs the approval of the local authority. Ashdown Forest is a notable example where the local authority has approved a special Wealdway waymark post for the Forest area suitable for use on open ground.

The Wealdway route runs in some places along a country road without a pedestrian footpath. In such instances the rule is that you should walk on the right-hand side of the road facing oncoming traffic and, of course, keeping well in to your right. On right-handed blind bends it is advisable to move over to the left-hand side of the bend.

The Wealdway: a background

As you walk the Wealdway you can find, either on the path itself or very close to it, a kaleidoscope of detail that illumines in a fascinating way the 5000 year-old story of this part of south-east England.

If you wish to go back to primaeval times there is the hamlet of Swanscombe – although this is a little way off the path – only 2 miles west of Gravesend, which has given the name to 'Swanscombe Man'. Here skull fragments of an 'inhabitant of Kent' of a quarter of a million years ago were found in a quarry in 1935 by an amateur archaeologist, and are now to be seen in the Natural History Museum in South Kensington. Sussex's matching effort was the discovery 150 years ago in Tilgate Forest in the Weald near Crawley, 9 miles west of the Wealdway, again by an amateur, of the first fossil Iguanodon, 150 million years old!

But the walker quite rightly will be more interested in what he can discover closer at hand, and the earliest finds are from Neolithic times (New Stone age – about 3000 years ago). By the side of the path, just where the sandy soil of the Weald begins, after you have dropped down from the crest of the North Downs, there are the Coldrum Stones of a Neolithic burial chamber in which 22 skeletons were found and, a mile farther south, the Long Barrow at Addington from the same period. On the last section of the path, in Sussex, is the 'causewayed camp' on the top of Combe Hill, where Neolithic dwellers on the South Downs 'corralled' their cattle: they were the first to turn from hunting to rear cattle, pigs and sheep and to grow crops – you could say they were the first examples of 'civilised man'.

Recorded history begins with the Roman occupation. Caesar, after landing on his punitive expedition of 55 BC, soon came up against the barrier presented by the thick forest of the Weald that stretched from Pevensey for 90 miles westwards, named by them Anderida. He tells how the Britons used the woods to mount quite successful ambushes on his troops. For us on the Wealdway, however, it is the traces of the occupation of the Romans dating from Claudius' invasion of 42 AD that arouse interest. The path closely follows in places the line of the Lewes–London road, one of those – the other was the Brighton–London road – built by the Romans to serve the iron-works they opened up in the Weald. Of the many Roman foundry sites in the Weald, the one near Fairwarp on Ashdown Forest is very close to the path. At Camp Hill, also on Ashdown, you can see traces of the Roman road only 50 m from the route. Modern archaeological excavations are still discovering Roman iron-workings in the Weald: one at Garden Hill near Wych Cross has recently revealed a Romano–British dwelling with a bath-house on the foundry site; and from another one, at Bardown near Wadhurst, it has been calculated that 10,000 tons of iron were produced during its existence in the second and third centuries.

For geographical reasons Kent north of the Weald was the region most developed by the Romans in southern England. It was closest to Gaul (France), their largest colony and military base; it was fertile and was able to supply London, which was soon made their capital. The main road, Watling Street, was built without delay to connect Dover, Canterbury and Rochester with the capital. When you are in Gravesend, the museum is worth a visit: there you will find some of the exhibits from excavations of the Roman Vagniacae at Springhead, $2\frac{1}{2}$ miles west of Gravesend, only discovered in 1964 when the building of a re-alignment of the A2 (Watling Street) was taking place. In contrast to Kent, the only settlements of any size in Sussex were Chichester and the fortified port of Pevensey, although the Romans found the coastal strip a pleasant place to live in. Many villa sites have been found there, as well as the 'palace' of a Romano–British king at Fishbourne just west of Chichester. On the Wealdway, in addition to the Roman road and iron-workings in Ashdown Forest, there is the connection where the minor Roman Pevensey–Lewes road crosses the path south of Arlington.

According to the Venerable Bede, writing 300 years after the events, Kent was occupied by the Teutonic Jutes after the departure of the Romans and Sussex was taken by the South Saxons. It is thought that the Jutes came from the mid-Rhine area and the South Saxons from farther south. The development of Saxon Kent and of

Saxon Sussex ('Saxon' is used here for the whole period up to the Norman Conquest) was quite different and produced a diversity in speech, manners and customs and even, until recently, in laws. The main reason was the lack of communication and this becomes obvious if you look at the 'Domesday' maps found in those mines of information, the Victoria Series of County Histories. These maps show all the Saxon villages and settlements figuring in the Normans' survey, the Domesday Book of 1086. There is only one settlement, Rotherfield, shown in the whole of a 20-mile wide strip of country astride of the Kent–Sussex border. This strip is the High Weald, showing that there had been hardly any clearance done in the 500 years after the Romans had left. Actually, there were a few 'pockets' in the forests now shown in Domesday: some Kentish manors and the big ecclesiastical landlords, for example, abbeys, owned pig-pastures on the Weald where the pigs were taken each summer to feed off the acorns. Villages in Kent ending in -den have their origin in this way.

Another difference was in the realm of religion. Ethelbert, King of Kent, had as his queen Bertha, Christian daughter of the King of Paris. She persuaded her husband to send to the famous Pope Gregory and ask for missionaries to be sent to Kent. Gregory sent Augustine, who arrived with his band of monks in 596 in Ethelbert's capital, Canterbury. Not long after, Ethelbert was baptised and soon the whole of Kent was christianised. The story of the conversion of Sussex is quite different. Augustine's mission had no effect on the Sussex people; probably they did not hear of it. It was not until nearly 100 years later, in 680, according to tradition, that Wilfrid, a monk from York, came down to Sussex to work among them. The missions of Augustine and Wilfrid were in complete contrast. Augustine, combining a missionary zeal and a talent for organisation, with the prestige of the whole Roman church supporting him, proceeded to divide Kent and the nearby area into dioceses, the foundation of church organisation in Britain to this day. Wilfrid, on the other hand, was a monk of the Iona and Holy Island tradition. The monks of the north were pastors more than organisers and by settling among the people won them to the faith by devotion and example. So effective was Wilfrid's work and that of later Sussex saints, St Cuthman and St Richard of Chichester, that the Sussex people were given the name 'silly Sussex', a corruption of 'Selig (holy) Sussex'.

The inhabitants of Kent[1] were known from early days for their rugged independence. There is a legend that after the Battle of Hastings the men of Kent rallied their own forces, barred William the Conqueror's way to London, and, catching him in an awkward spot strategically, forced from him the promise that he would respect their laws and customs. This is not difficult to believe as there was one law, peculiar to Kent, that of 'gavelkind' that was only removed from the statute book in 1925! Under 'gavelkind' the estate of any man dying without leaving a will was divided equally among all his sons and did not fall to the eldest, as in the rest of the country. One can quite see how this could over the years produce a number of small landowners, proud and stubborn. The 'Kentish Yeoman' does seem to have been rather a special type: I cannot recall having seen as many inn-signs for 'The Devon Yeoman' or 'The Norfolk Yeoman' as I have for 'The Kentish Yeoman' but I may be biased, being a 'Kentish Man' myself! But is it a coincidence that it was a Kent man, Wat Tyler, who spearheaded the great Rising of 1381 and with John Ball and the others from Kent captured the Tower of London and the City?

What has the Wealdway to show of Saxon England? A unique example is Luddesdown Court in Kent, right on the Wealdway, thought from its features to have been built by Saxon craftsmen about the year 1100, working under Norman direction. Only the early doorway can be seen from the outside. Other features are inside and the house is not open to the public, but just looking at a house that has been lived in for nearly 900 years is quite an experience.

Sussex has fewer than twenty Saxon churches, i.e. those built before the Norman Conquest. Some are almost completely Saxon, others retain much of their Saxon character. Of these treasures there are two on the Wealdway: Arlington and Jevington churches.

[1] For the uninitiated, those born in Kent are traditionally divided into two groups: the 'Men of Kent', those born south of the Medway, and the 'Kentish Men', those born north of the river.

Arlington could possibly have been built on a pagan sacred site. Undoubtedly many more of the churches we see on the Wealdway are successors of earlier Saxon churches but these would have been wooden buildings; it is in the character of 'holy Sussex' that the people had in so many cases invested in the more costly stone.

It is important to remember that the layout of most of the old villages we pass through on the Wealdway was established in Saxon times: the village church, the manor and the larger farms probably occupied the same positions as they do today, 1000 years later. Their names in the vast majority of cases are Anglo-Saxon ('Old English').

In Norman times it was the castles and the powerful ecclesiastical foundations, cathedrals, abbeys, priories and so on, that dominated the life of the countryside. You have on the Wealdway the splendid castle at Tonbridge. Many of the abbeys and priories were utterly destroyed under the Dissolution of 1539 but others were presented or sold to Henry VIII's cronies who made magnificent residences out of them. You can get a vivid picture of a ruined priory converted into a Tudor country house at Michelham Priory, right on the Wealdway and also from the smaller but equally fascinating Wilmington Priory.

The Middle Ages have much to show: there are some magnificent churches to be seen dating from the twelfth century onwards. Each one is noted in the text but among the larger ones Cobham, Chiddingly and Alfriston and, of the smaller, Withyham and Buxted are of particular interest. From the history and monuments you can piece together the lives of those who worshipped in them over the years. What better picture of feminine fashions from the fourteenth to the sixteenth centuries could you wish for than that portrayed on the brasses in Cobham church – the largest collection in any English church? Who could fail to be impressed by the record of Church-warden Pitcher's family of Hellingly, who claimed to have lived in the parish for 500 years?

Apart from the mediaeval churches along the Wealdway there are the splendid timbered manor houses, outward signs of the growing wealth and power of England. Penshurst Place is the most

famous, others you can only admire from the outside or take a
picture of. Examples are Horselunges Manor and Stonehill and
many superb smaller houses: the yeoman's houses at Bullingstone
and the one at Sole Street (the latter, belonging to the National
Trust, can be visited with special permission). Of the more lowly
dwellings there is the perfect fourteenth-century Clergy House at
Alfriston, the National Trust's earliest acquisition.

The Middle Ages saw the rise of the great landowning families,
for example the Pelhams in Sussex (the Pelham 'buckle' sign is to be
seen in the churches of East Hoathly and Chiddingly, among
others). That their lands were wide-spread and that the family had
its troubles one can gather from a moving letter written from
Pevensey Castle by Lady Joan Pelham at the time of the Peasant
Rising of 1381, one of the earliest surviving letters in the English
langauge. I quote from Esther Meynell's *Sussex*, a delightful book.

My dear Lord – I recommend me to your high Lordship, with
heart and body and all my poor might. And with all this I thank
you as my dear Lord, dearest and best beloved of all earthly
lords. I say for me, and thank you, my dear Lord, with all this
that I said before of your comfortable letter that you sent me
from Pontefract, that came to me on Mary Magdalene's day: for
by my troth I was never so glad as when I heard by your letter
that ye were strong enough with the grace of God for to keep you
from the malice of your enemies. And, dear Lord, if it like to
your high Lordship that as soon as ye might that I might hear of
your gracious speed, which God Almighty continue and increase.
And, my dear Lord, if it like you to know my fare, I am here laid
by in mannr of a siege with the county of Sussex, Surrey and a
great parcel of Kent, so that I may not out nor no victuals get me,
but with much hard. Wherefore, my dear, if it like you by the
advice of your wise counsel for to set remedy for the salvation of
your Castle and withstand the malice of the shires aforesaid. And
also that ye be despitefully wrought to you, and to your Castle, to
your men and to your tenants; for this country have they wasted
for a great while.

Farewell, my dear Lord; the Holy Trinity keep you from your

enemies and soon send me good tidings of you.

Written at Pevensey, in the Castle, on St Jacob's day last past.

By your own poor
J. Pelham

To my true Lord

The Middle Ages saw the revival of the Wealden iron industry. There does not seem to have been any industry in Saxon times although there is a mention in the Domesday Book of a possible foundry at East Grinstead. It is from the thirteenth century that the industry begins to appear in the records. Particularly intriguing are the accounts for the years from 1329–34 and 1350–4 of the iron-works belonging to the Lady of Clare at Tudeley, a village near Tonbridge. Here we have a full list of the income and expenses with the costs of fuel, wages, etc. From the accounts it can be seen that the wages almost doubled over the two periods, due no doubt to the intervention of the Black Death in 1349, resulting in a shortage of labour. For the hot work there was one penny a week for beer money, divided among the four furnacemen!

The industry continued to grow until by the fifteenth century there were probably 100 foundries in the Weald.

For walkers of the Wealdway there is the site at Oldlands near Fairwarp in Ashdown Forest where the Roman works were later revived. Here the iron for the first British cannon was produced. On the recommended $3\frac{1}{2}$ mile diversion from Gun Hill near Chiddingly there is the site of Stream Mill to be seen as well as the nearby splendid seventeenth-century Stream Farm, probably built by the French family, famous iron-founders and owners of the mill. Also on the Wealdway route is Buxted church, whose Parson Levett was responsible, with 'his servant', Ralph Hogg, for making the first cannon in 1543. As the local saying ran:

Master Huggett (Hogg) and his man John
They did make the first can-non.

Hogg House, at the entrance of Buxted Park and also on the path, shows that he did well out of it. Those who have visited Kipling's

home, Bateman's, at Burwash will have seen another lovely
iron-founder's house built from the proceeds of the iron-works close
by.

As mentioned in the text, the historian Hume noted that the
Wealden cannon were the best in the world. They certainly
commanded a high price: Sussex smugglers did a brisk illegal trade
with the Continent, selling cannon to enemies and friends! The
cannon-makers' secret is not known: Straker's standard work,
Wealden Iron, states that it may have been the quality of the iron or
the moulds in which the cannon were cast, or perhaps the Wealden
clay made the best moulds.[1]

When you walk past Oldlands Corner through Furnace Wood or
stop to look down on the mill-race at Stream Mill, all in perfect
country settings of green pasture and woodland glade, it is hard to
imagine that for two or three hundred years these were the scenes of
roaring, smoking furnaces with the din of huge clanking hammers
and much bustle and shouting as massive iron cannon were loaded
on to creaking wagons, to be drawn by slow-moving teams of oxen
over muddy tracks to the river Ouse. It is as though some mighty
magician has waved an all-powerful wand and, hey presto, all the
man-made paraphernalia of iron-making has disappeared without a
trace leaving the fields and forests untouched.

Ashdown Forest is one of the highlights of the Wealdway. As you
leave Withyham behind and enter Five Hundred Acre Wood
through Fisher's Gate you have a $1\frac{1}{2}$ mile walk through woodland of
oak and beech much the same as covered what is now the bare
upland of Ashdown Forest. The robbing of the timber for fuel for
the iron industry and the building of homes and ships over the
centuries has taken its toll, but it is superb walking country. It is a
fascinating thought that to build a man-of-war 2000 oak trees had to
be felled. To take the fleet at the Armada, with 25 galleons and 65
smaller ships, all armed with hundreds of cannon, the quantity of
timber required to make the ships and to fuel the furnaces smelting

[1] Those interested may like to know there are Wealden cannon preserved in the Tower
of London. Two of particular note are by the archway leading to the History Gallery:
they have 'JF', the initials of John Fuller of Heathfield, on the 'trunnion'. There are two
others from the Weald in the Royal Fusiliers Museum section of the Tower.

the iron for the cannon must have been colossal! Not all the timber came from Sussex, of course; there were the Forest of Dean and other sources.

Perhaps the most interesting feature of Ashdown Forest is the jurisdiction over the area of the Board of Conservators whereby the 'Commoners' or residents of the Forest exercise the rights they have been jealously guarding for 700 years. Nowadays their chief efforts are directed towards seeing that this marvellous stretch of open country is preserved for the use and enjoyment of an appreciative public. Good examples of their activities are the special 'Ashdown Forest' waymarks provided for the Wealdway – the best on the whole route.

During the eighteenth century it was decided that coal was better for iron-smelting and with iron ore also available with the coal in the north the industry moved there and has stayed there ever since.

Transport conditions in parts of the Weald must have been dreadful right up to the early days of the last century. It was a common saying that Sussex women were unusually long in the leg, having to wade through so much mud. Defoe from his travels wrote in 1724 that conditions were so bad that he had seen a tree from an ox cart with twenty oxen having to be left by the roadside through the rains so that it sometimes took two or three years to get it to Chatham! One lady took a six-ox cart to get to church because the road was so bad: let us hope she had not far to go! Apparently, oxen with their hooves were better able to negotiate the mud but it must have been very slow. We can be grateful that our modern roads (and good footpaths) enable us to explore the Wealden countryside so easily nowadays.

To be on foot in the Medway valley at a certain time of the year is to enjoy a unique experience: a Kentish orchard in April is a breathtaking sight and on the Wealdway between West Peckham and the Medway you are surrounded in places by a sea of white and pink blossom. It is fascinating to learn that the conversion of Kent to intensive fruit-growing, earning for the county the title of The Garden of England, was due to one man: a certain Richard Harrys, 'fruiterer' to King Henry VIII. Although the historian Pliny (23–79 AD) mentions that the Romans brought cherries to Britain there had been no growing of fruit on any scale except by monasteries. Harrys in 1533 bought 100 acres at Teynham near Faversham and 'with great care and no small labour brought from beyond the seas the sweet cherry, the temperate pippin and the golden reinette' (another type of apple). From these beginnings 30 more orchard holdings were developed, laying the foundation of the vast acreage of fruit trees seen today. I like to think of Richard Harrys as a typical Kentish yeoman, independent-minded and, in his case, with vision and expertise, quite in the tradition of the Englishman who started the Malayan rubber industry with plants from Brazil and the one who, according to some, took cottonseed to New England. How pleased he would be to see what a blessing his enterprise has turned out to be for his country and Britain. He is buried at Fordwich just north of Canterbury.

You are sure also to come across hop-gardens on the Wealdway: near West Peckham and Penshurst, for example. The wires strung on tall hop-poles are for the shoots or 'bines' that grow as much as 8 inches in a day. The 'flowers', the hops, used to give flavour to beer, are picked mechanically nowadays but up to a few years ago hundreds of hop-pickers used to come down in August and September from the East End of London to pick the hops and combine the earnings of a few extra pounds with a kind of holiday. Special trains with the poorest rolling-stock the railway could find would bring as many as 30,000 to the hop-gardens travelling mainly through the night, many of them whole families, sometimes with the children hidden in sacks to avoid paying fares! They lived in huts and tents, used by the same families year by year. Conditions improved with the passing of the years but the farmer could not do without his rowdy, humorous, hard-drinking Cockney hop-pickers. In the early days there were disasters, as when cholera broke out, or accidents such as the one at Hartlake Bridge near Tonbridge in 1853 when 35 were drowned.

The hop-pickers and other low-paid workers on the land are now figures of the past and the countryside is more prosperous for all concerned, but we can spare a thought for those farmers and farm-workers who for centuries have given their lives to keeping the land fruitful for us.

Natural life on the Wealdway

Apart from its historical associations, the country through which the Wealdway passes is rich in natural life, particularly birds, butterflies and flowers. Wild flowers of many kinds are to be found in abundance all along the path and the North and South Downs are the home of more than one kind of wild orchid. The south-east of England is the breeding place, and, in migration times, the resting place, for more species of birds than any other part of the country and on the Wealdway the bird-watcher can get some memorable surprises if he or she keeps a sharp lookout. Two experiences I treasure are hearing for the first time the song of the redstart as well as watching the bird for some minutes feeding from the flies in the evening near Fairwarp, and being able to record the song of a nightingale during the afternoon near Arlington. I could not see him as he was in bushes on the other side of the Cuckmere but I was content enough with his song, at such an unusual time. There are butterflies too – I remember in particular two beautiful Comma butterflies on the path alongside a hop-garden near Penshurst (hop plants are their favourite place for egg-laying).

I hope these few background notes will serve to add interest and enjoyment to your walking on the Wealdway and perhaps stimulate a deeper study, with the aid of the bibliography, of the many features that in the space available I have only been able to touch upon. It is sure to be infinitely rewarding.

Gravesend (Tollgate Moat House, A2) to **Wrotham Heath**
$11\frac{1}{2}$ miles

General description

As the Wealdway starts on the A2 2 miles south of the Thames at
Gravesend, there is no need to visit the town itself before setting out
to walk the path, but it is worthwhile to do so. Although it has a
history covering 1000 years you will not find in Gravesend rows of
quaint half-timbered houses: they have gone long ago – a disastrous
fire in 1727 practically destroyed the old town – but like most
waterside towns it still has atmosphere. During the week it is a
bustling, lively place and if you are there on a fine day an hour or
two could be well spent watching the river scene from the Fort
Gardens.

In the first 10 miles of the Wealdway, starting from the A2, you
have a foretaste of the variety encountered along the whole 80
miles. After crossing a couple of miles of flat arable land and
orchards you enter a landscape of chalk hill and valley, woodland
and pasture, dotted with prosperous farmhouses, each with its oast
house or two. Continue through the village of Sole Street – its
railway station is a useful jumping-off place for the long-distance
path – and then over rolling country to Luddesdown, whose manor
house is reputed to be the oldest continuously lived-in habitation in
the south. For the next 3 miles the scene of sloping green fields on
either side of the route delights the eye. The path gradually climbs
through a plantation, Whitehorse Wood, bringing you to the edge of
the 198 m (650 ft) chalk escarpment of the North Downs before
crossing the North Downs Way and the Pilgrims' Way at the foot.
This is a good spot to rest and enjoy the wide view of the Medway
valley before you descend the steep path – in late April a mass of
primroses.

After crossing the Pilgrims' Way, the Wealdway follows an
ancient track taking you in a few minutes past one of the most

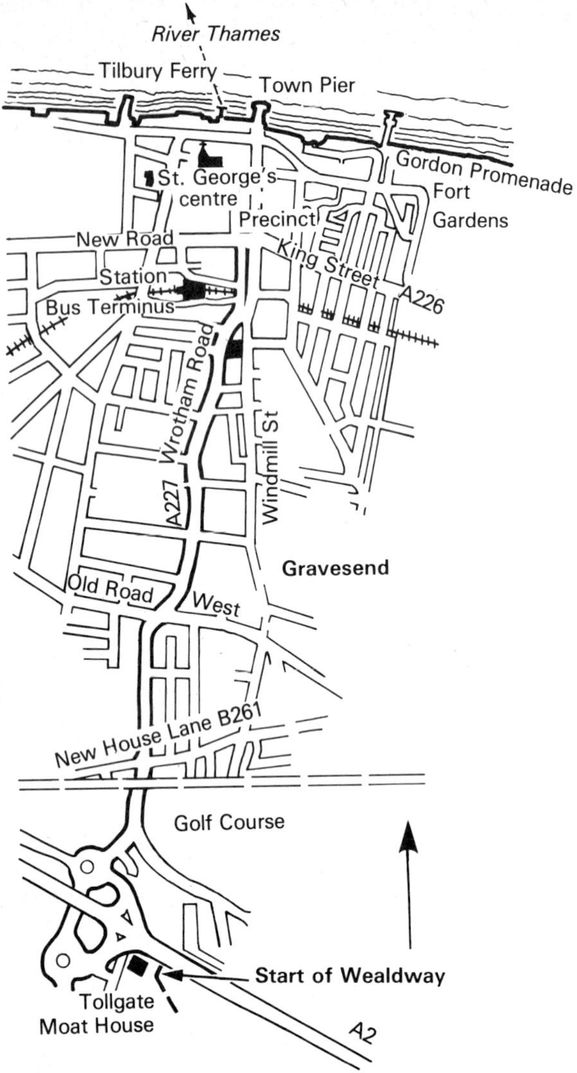

River Thames

Tilbury Ferry — Town Pier

St. George's centre

Gordon Promenade

Fort Gardens

New Road

Precinct

Station

King Street A226

Bus Terminus

Wrotham Road

Windmill St

A227

Gravesend

Old Road West

New House Lane B261

Golf Course

Start of Wealdway

Tollgate Moat House

A2

significant archaeological sites in Kent: the Coldrum Long Barrow, a large Neolithic 'chamber tomb' owned by the National Trust. In another mile, through a pleasant wood, sheltering in the spring and early summer a variety of wild flowers, the M20 is reached, close to the junctions with the M26 and the A20. The path crosses under the M20 and close to the attractive village of Addington.

Addington is one of the number of villages and monuments which, while not lying on the path itself, can be visited by making short diversions – varying in distance from a few hundres metres to a couple of miles each way. Apart from Addington, other recommended diversions in this section are (from north to south) Cobham – particularly interesting, Nurstead and Trottiscliffe. You will find descriptions and sketch maps of the diversions on pages 53–65.

MAPS
OS 1:50 000 177, 188
OS 1:25 000 TQ 67/77, 66/76, 65/75

Gravesend (Old English 'Groves end')
The Domesday Book records a settlement at 'Gravesham' and also a more valuable one at 'Meltone' with a 'hithe' (haven). This is the present Milton, the eastern part of Gravesend. There was a church at Milton, noted by the Domesday scribe. The two sites were the first solid ground providing a landing place after entering the Thames estuary, both the south bank of the river below Gravesend and the opposite shore being too marshy. 'Gravesham' has been the name since 1974 for the new borough including Northfleet to the west. The Romans knew the area: there are traces of Roman occupation at Northfleet and the Roman road, Watling Street, between Dover and London is now the A2 only 2 miles away. From early days Gravesend developed into a port where passengers and goods could be transferred into smaller boats and taken upriver to London. This would avoid some tricky navigation hazards and the danger of running on a sandbank. From the time Alfred the Great revived London after the Dark Ages there was probably quite a traffic in both passengers and produce between London and the

Gravesend Reach, River Thames

country's ecclesiastical capital, Canterbury, and the fertile land around, making use of Gravesend.

In Norman times the practices and privileges of the watermen of Gravesend were described as 'going back to time immemorial'; in the Middle Ages there are records of English kings, including Henry VIII, and foreign notables, often with huge retinues of richly-apparelled followers, landing en route to London. The town's oldest building, the thirteenth-century Milton Chantry down by the river, was part of a twelfth-century hospital – indicating a place of some importance 800 years ago.

We get a more detailed picture of Gravesend in the seventeenth century. Samuel Pepys in his Diary mentions the town 23 times and certainly knew it very well. His job as Clerk to the Acts of the Navy Board entailed many visits to 'his ships' lying at Chatham. He usually went by boat from the Tower of London, where his office was, to Gravesend and thence by horseback or sometimes coach to Rochester or Chatham. Among the town's many inns The Ship seems his favourite. Mine Host of The Ship was quite a source of useful information. The inn was at the bottom of the High Street by the river but disappeared long ago. We also read of Pepys being 'very merry' at The Swan when he met an old waterman friend, Doncaster, for supper one August evening in 1662. On a June day in 1665 he sent his wife, her maid and his faithful clerk, Hewer, down to Gravesend for a day's outing. (Gravesend was a resort for Londoners right up to the end of the last century. The gardens of Rosherville offered coloured lights, fireworks and concerts.) Caught by a thunderstorm the party didn't get home until 5 a.m. Pepys strikes a sombre note on the same day, having seen a red cross on a door in Drury Lane: ten weeks later he writes, 'late in the dark to Gravesend where great is the plague and I troubled so long to wait for the tide.' The watermen were not always as friendly as Doncaster: Pepys was most upset when one tried to charge him twenty shillings to take some horses across the river. He comments that he threatened to send him to sea 'and I will do it' – one way of recruiting crews for the Royal Navy!

The Dutch attack on the Medway fleet in 1667, when they burned three men-of-war and towed away the Royal Charles, was a worrying time for Pepys: he went down at once to Gravesend where mine host of The Ship told him how people fleeing had brought their goods down to his cellars for safety; the boom of cannon could be clearly heard.

A diary entry for a calm day in September 1665 gives an insight not only into how the Gravesend poor lived in those days but into

Pepys' generous character. A lover of good food, he obviously kept his eyes open for a bargain; on the way to Chatham by river he fell in with a fishing boat who sold him 'a great deal of fish'. He called in at Gravesend to have it dressed at a place called Whites and afterwards was taken to a low tavern in the poor part of the town where he found 'two wretched dirty seamen' who had some precious spices for sale, filched from a prize taken by the naval ship on which they had served. Samuel bought 37 lb of cloves and 10 lb of nutmegs, giving them more than they were asking: 'but Lord! to see how silly these men are in the selling of it and easy to be persuaded to anything!'

Gravesend continued to grow. More and more shipping in the Thames, including troopships, deposited or embarked passengers and cargoes. The coming of the railway in the 1840s gave another boost. One man who made his home here from 1869 to 1871 was the famous Royal Engineer Colonel (later General) 'Chinese' Gordon, who gained a reputation by leading the Empress of China's troops armed only with a cane. He supervised the defences at Gravesend first erected by Henry VIII in 1539 where now the Fort Gardens are laid out (his house was destroyed by a flying bomb in 1944). Gordon was killed in Khartoum by fanatics in 1885 and became a folk hero. While in Gravesend he spent much of his time and money helping the poor boys of the neighbourhood, seeing that they were adequately fed and clothed and received schooling.

In the 1880s, pending the completion of Tilbury Docks, Gravesend was the terminal port for the P & O steamers plying weekly between the UK and India and the Far East, the passengers going out by tender from the town pier to the ships lying in the Thames.

Shipping later declined but industries including paper, cement and electric cables supported progress in the town. One link with the town's Victorian times is the large number of Indian families settled there, descended from the crews of ships on the Indian and Far Eastern runs. The number of shops selling Indian goods, silks, brassware, foods and so on, is astonishing.

Route Southbound
Those arriving at Gravesend by ferry from the Essex shore from
Tilbury, and the enthusiasts who wish to walk every foot of the way
from Thames to the English Channel, should turn left from the ferry
pier down West Street and then right up the High Street – at least
700 years old and now a paved pedestrian precinct. None of the
buildings that Pepys would have known have survived but on the
left is the frontage of massive classical pillars of the former Town
Hall built in 1836 also providing the entrance to the Market, a busy
place on a Saturday. On the left of the pillar entrance, housed in the
former police station, is the museum, small but most interesting,
particularly for the finds from the Roman site at Springhead
(Vagniacae) only $2\frac{1}{2}$ miles away, discovered when the A2 was being
widened in 1964. One of the treasures found was a hoard of over
400 silver and gold Roman coins – they were declared treasure
trove and a good proportion of the value handed over to the
workmen. Museum opening hours are 2–5 p.m. weekdays except
Wednesdays; 9 a.m.–1 p.m. Saturdays.

Gravesend Parish Church, a typical eighteenth-century building,
replacing the previous fifteenth-century church burnt in the 1727
fire, can be seen from West Street. It is of special interest to
American visitors as in the chancel is buried Pocohontas, daughter
of an Indian chief of Virginia who married an English settler, came
over with her husband and was presented at the court of James I in
1616. On her way home she died in Gravesend. The statue of her in
the churchyard is a replica of one in Jamestown, Virginia, USA.

To join the Wealdway 2 miles away, on emerging from the High
Street, turn right into New Road, the main shopping thoroughfare
and then first left. This will bring you to Stone Street; you then
proceed as in (*b*) below. The official start of the Wealdway is found
on the south side of the A2 (Watling Street) a few metres from the
intersection with the A227 (Gravesend–Meopham–Tonbridge
road) near the Tollgate Moat House.

(a) *Car travellers using the A2*
Take the A227 turn-off (south direction – 'Meopham'). On the left

(east) just south of the flyover will be seen the free public parking area. Starting your walk from the car-park, make for the Tollgate Moat House; follow the footway encircling their private carpark area. As you come along-side the A2 you will see on your right (south) a stile with the Wealdway WW waymark, surmounting the low grass embankment: this is the start of the 80 miles through to Eastbourne.

(b) *On foot or by public transport from Gravesend*
The Tollgate Moat House is linked by daily bus service from the Gravesend bus station (opposite the railway station). On alighting at the bus stop make for the footway passing under the A2 (on the right-hand side of the roundabout). On emerging from the underpass follow the footpath immediately on your left leading in the direction of the Tollgate Moat House on to the footway alongside the south side of the A2, then proceed as above.

If walking from Gravesend railway station or bus station turn right over the railway (Stone Street), carry straight on and bear right at the island site with the impressive Civic Centre. You are now on the Wrotham Road, the A227 and a 1¾ mile walk to the Tollgate Moat House.

After crossing the stile – the WW waymark will often prove a welcome guide on the next 80 miles – the path carries on for a few metres inside the Moat House fence to a gate in the fence. Go through this gate and your path continues diagonally ahead across the large field. Should the field be ploughed up or bearing crops and the line not clear make for the left-hand tree of the line of small trees on the skyline to the right (the fingerpost marked 'Ifield' does not show the correct direction: it should be a good bit to the left). After crossing the field you come out on a wide farm track bordered on the left by an orchard. Turn right along this track and keep straight on for 1¼ miles. There are two kinks in the track but maintain your direction. On the left at the first kink is the eighteenth-century farmhouse, Ifield Court.

For the diversion to Cobham*, a village of exceptional interest, turn left off the Wealdway passing in front of Ifield Court (see page 53 and sketch map).

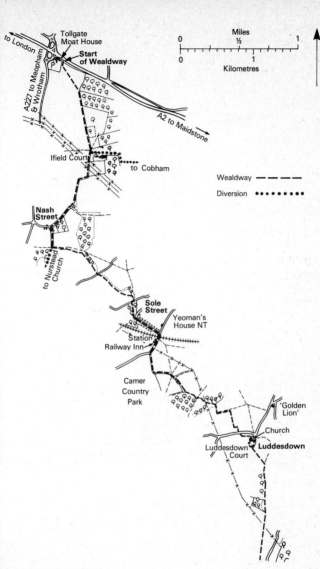

(see page 41 for continuation)

Ifield Court near Nash Street

Continuing on the Wealdway the track emerges on a narrow metalled road at the hamlet of Nash Street, a quiet backwater with a cluster of cottages. Turn left along the road which in 200 m is barred by a wooden field gate.

The field gate is the start of a footpath (although there is no sign)

The Wealdway near Nash Street

across the field for a diversion to Nurstead Church, for those interested in old churches (see page 61 and sketch map).

Immediately on the left of the field gate is a Wealdway stile. The path leads from the stile past a small copse, down a dip and over two more stiles. Follow the path to the right where it bends along the field. Carry on along the edge of the field: you come out on to a minor road. Cross straight over and continue on the footpath signed to 'Sole Street'. 500 m along the footpath there is a waymarked stile in a field fence on the left; cross this stile, and the path leads diagonally across the field to another stile, bringing you on to a road. Turn right and on the opposite side of the road, in a few metres, will be seen an unmarked path on the left leading through woodland. This skirts the gardens of a line of bungalows. Turn left where the path makes a T-junction with another path at the end of the wood and you emerge on to a residential road (Manor Road, Sole Street). Turn right to the junction with the main B2009 road. Immediately on the left of the T-junction is the Tudor Yeoman's House (National Trust) – a typical sixteenth-century Kentish timbered house. To visit the house a written application has to be made to the occupier: address this to 'Yeoman's House, Sole Street, Cobham, Kent'. There is a village shop nearby.

To rejoin the Wealdway, turn right along the B2009 at the T-junction, past Sole Street railway station (a useful jumping-off point for the Way) and the Railway Inn (meals and snacks daily including Sundays). 300 m down the road, on the left, is the entrance to the Camer Country Park.

Camer Country Park is a large and open place suitable for picnics and other recreations. There are toilets, but no refreshment facilities.

At the left-hand side of the Country Park entrance is a wide farm track between two white posts (concrete footpath sign) running along the eastern boundary of the park. This is the continuation of the Wealdway. Follow the track which bends to the left after about 500 m, passing an isolated cottage. Maintain the direction at the junction with other marked footpaths, your path climbing the slope ahead and entering the patch of woodland in the left-hand (eastern) corner of the field on the crest of the slope. The crest provides a good sheltered spot for a rest if you can ignore the pylons dominating the view.

The Wealdway near Nurstead Court

After a few metres through the copse the path emerges at a field
stile. Turn sharp right over the stile and descend the steep slope to
another stile in a wire fence. Here turn left, the line of the path
running parallel with the wire fence and the few trees. You may
want to pause here to admire the view – one of the finest in Kent,
with the hamlet of Luddesdown in the valley below among the trees
to the left. Continuing, you cross another wire fence and, following

Luddesdown from the Wealdway looking north – Luddesdown Court to the left of the church

the sign, turn right descending the slope, turning left when you reach yet another wire fence across your path. At the field boundary turn down the slope once more – there is a yellow waymark on a powerline post – and on to the narrow metalled road at the bottom of the valley. The official path proceeds up some steps on the bank on the opposite side of the road, across a stile and left along the field edge to more steps down to the road by the entrance to Luddesdown church. Alternatively you can walk along the road for the short distance involved.

Scenically and historically Luddesdown is one of the gems of the Wealdway. Church, manor, farm and schoolhouse, sheltered among noble trees, form a perfect picture. The site has been a first choice from very early times: traces have been found of Stone and Iron Age dwellings and, on the northern slopes, Roman pottery. Of intense interest is Luddesdown Court adjoining the church, one of the oldest continuously lived-in homes in the country. The doorway is nearly 900 years old and inside there are a number of features almost as ancient, including a thirteenth-century fireplace. The house is not open to visitors. Luddesdown is mentioned in the Domesday Book as having a church: the present one is largely a nineteenth-century restoration but parts of the Norman building remain in the tower, the arch of the chancel and the south door, and there is a fifteenth-century brass. For refreshment, the pub, The Golden Lion, is in Lower Luddesdown, 500 m up the road running north from the church. Snacks (cheese or ham rolls) are available on weekdays.

Continue round the churchyard wall with the farmyard barn on your right. Cross the signposted stile in the wire fence on your left and go straight ahead climbing the slope (sign 'FP 228'). Go between the two field gates and follow the line of trees on the field boundary to your right; make for the stile at the end of the trees descending the slope; go through a gap in the fence and on to the stile to be seen in the long wire fence ahead. The wide valley with tree-crested slopes opening in front of you, with a typical Kentish farmhouse in the distance, will tempt you to stop and enjoy the view. Over the stile, the path descends diagonally down to the far corner of the large field and on to the road. Turn right and take the right fork, passing Great Buckland Farm.

200 m past the farm up the hill, on the left is your footpath with a gate and stile. Follow this path, first skirting and then entering the wood (Luxon Wood) – a mass of primroses in the spring. When

Great Buckland Farm

emerging from the wood bear right diagonally across the field
towards the prominent beech tree, then left along the field edge.
Carry on along the track – which is part of a bridle-way – with a wire
fence on the right. This bit of bridle-way can be very muddy if there
has been recent rain. On reaching the roadway turn left passing
Boughurst Street Farm on your left. Where the road starts to bend

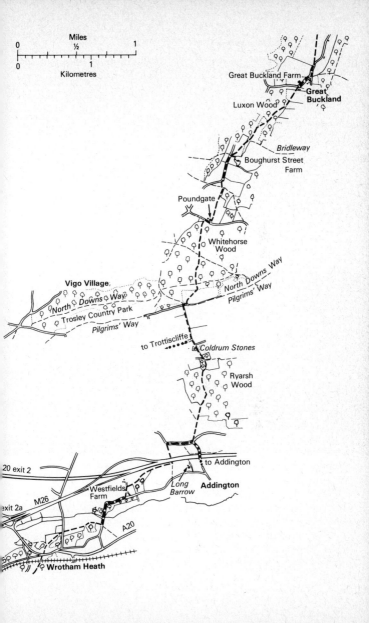

Looking south from the North Downs at the edge of Whitehorse Wood

to the right enter the iron field gate on your left; follow the field
boundary for 100 m and then go through an open gate on the left.
Turn sharp right and keep straight on with a copse on your left
across the field until you come to a farm with a stile giving on to a
road. Turn right on the road for a few metres to join the path on the
left through a wood (Whitehorse Wood). After 900 m you suddenly

emerge on the crest of the North Downs with a wide panorama of the fields, orchards and woods of the Weald stretching into the distance – another good place for a rest.

The path descends steeply down the chalk escarpment – in April this can be fringed with an unbelievable profusion of primroses – a true 'primrose path'. At the bottom of the slope is the junction with the Pilgrims' Way, here part of the official North Downs Way. Turn right along the Pilgrims' Way for a few metres.

The North Downs Way leaves the Pilgrims' Way, on the right, and climbs through the Trosley Country Park which extends for almost a mile westwards: an attractive woodland area with a car park and toilets at the western end (no refreshment facilities).

On the left of the Pilgrims' Way will be seen the NT sign to the Coldrum Long Barrow. This is the continuation of the Wealdway; 500 m down the path and on the right is a footpath leading to Trottiscliffe.

The Norman church of Trottiscliffe* (pronounced 'Trosley') is 900 m down the path on the right and is well worth seeing (see page 00 and sketch map); the village is 700 m further on. Just past the path to Trottiscliffe, right on the Wealdway, is the Coldrum Long Barrow. Owned by the National Trust, this is one of the most important archaeological sites in Kent. It is what is left of a 30 m long 'chamber tomb' from Neolithic (New Stone Age) times – 2500–3000BC. With other similar sites, Addington (see below) and Kit's Coty near Aylesford, they form part of the 'Medway culture'. The tombs had the huge stones for walls and roof and are thought to have been for a chieftain and his descendants – a kind of family vault. These in Kent are simimar to others in Germany and the Netherlands and could have been erected by invaders from those areas. They are all near ancient trackways, Coldrum and Addington near tracks leading from the east along and at the foot of the North Downs – the present North Downs Way and the Pilgrims' Way.

Coldrum Long Barrow, near Trottiscliffe

It is an intriguing thought that parts of the Wealdway nearby could also have been in use for 5000 years or more, perhaps before Britain was separated from the Continent! The 'sarsen stones' are blocks of sandstone that occur locally. The site is dedicated to Benjamin Harrison, grocer's son from nearby Ightham who last century found traces of prehistoric man at Oldbury Hill close to his village.

The North Downs from Coldrum Long Barrow

Continue southwards down the path entering a pleasant wood –
here, again, a haven for an abundance of spring flowers. Emerging
from the wood, go over two field stiles, the line of the path taking
you along the field boundary on your left and then to the right of a
farm shed seen ahead. You come out on a road; turn right along it –
there is a raised causeway on the north side for pedestrians.

Sandpits near Addington

The road going south from the T-junction across the motorway M20
leads (in 500 m) to the attractive village of Addington with an
archaeological site and old pub among other interesting features.
Another short diversion worth making (see page 000 and sketch
map).

The North Downs from the Wealdway near Wrotham Heath. In the foreground is the 16th century Ford Place

The Wealdway continues from the opposite (south) side of the road, along the far (west) fence of the quarry, 'Olley (Wrotham) Ltd'. There is a concrete footpath sign. The path leads under the motorway. Turn right immediately you emerge from under the bridge, climbing the embankment and keeping alongside the motorway fence. The path then turns away from the motorway up a short rise skirting a clump of trees and then proceeds diagonally over to Westfields Farm and on to the farm access road.

Turn left on the farm road and take the signed path almost immediately on the other side. This runs between two fences and leads to the minor road coming from Addington. Turn right and follow the road down to the bridge over a small stream; 100 m beyond the bridge, on the right, will be seen the footpath signed to Wrotham Heath. Follow this path that runs along the 'headland' (the farmer's term for the field edge) of a number of fields before reaching a minor road. This stretch of the Wealdway affords a fine view of the North Downs (and the M20!). Straight over the minor road, follow the signed path through the wood, with a small stream on the right. On a fine day in May this small spinney was alive with birds: in the 400 m I noted, among others, chichaff, green woodpecker, willow and long-tailed tits, blackcap, pheasant and magpie, and I only lingered for a minute or two. The path comes out on the busy A2 at Wrotham Heath.

Wrotham Heath (pronounced 'Root-ham'), not to be confused with Wrotham 2 miles to the north-west, is a small community lying along the main A20 road. There is a possibility that it is the successor to a settlement shown as Litel Broteham in the Domesday Book. Amenities include a Post Office, (open each weekday except Thursday afternoon and then 4–6 p.m.), a pub (the Royal Oak) and a restaurant. There is also accommodation (see list).

Route Northbound
To continue the Wealdway northwards from Wrotham Heath cross over the busy A20 (it is safer to cross by the traffic lights) and you will see the start of the path with sign and waymark almost opposite the Royal Oak pub. At first crossing a field, the route lies through a pleasant wood with a stream for about 400 m – a fine place for birds in the spring. When you come to a road cross over to the signed footpath at the side of the house 'The Nuttery'. The path follows the

'headland' (field edge) of a series of fields – with fine views of the North Downs – emerging at a road. Turn left down the hill, go over the bridge, up the hill the other side and round the bend. Just past the bungalow, Southfields, on the left of the road will be seen a waymarked path.

Diversion to the village of Addington* 1000 m down the road (see page 65 and sketch map).

Follow this narrow path between fences then turn left up the metalled farm road. Before reaching the farm there is a footpath on the right. This runs diagonally towards the M20 skirting the north edge of a clump of trees and continuing along the motorway fence. Turn left under the motorway bridge and along the path which leads to a road.

Diversion to Trottiscliffe* (see page 64 and sketch map).

At the roadway turn right past the sand quarry: go straight on at the T-junction (Woodgate Road) for a few metres and there is a waymark directing you northwards through a gap on the left in the hedgerow. Pass in front of the disused shed and proceed along the field boundary to the stile in the corner of the field. Go over this and the next stile ahead then through the wood (Ryarsh Wood), carpeted with a profusion of wild flowers in season. You emerge on a wide track continuing northwards.

In 300 m, beside the path, are the fascinating archaeological remains of the Coldrum Long Barrow* (page 43). A few metres further on the footpath from Trottiscliffe joins the track.

Keep going in the same direction and in 600 m you come to the junction with the Pilgrims' Way (North Downs Way) running east-west.

Trosley Country Park (see page 43 and sketch map).

Turn right on the Pilgrims' Way; almost immediately on the left are steps leading to the Wealdway path up the very steep North Downs chalk escarpment. A stiff ten-minute struggle brings its reward with the splendid views of the Medway valley from the top. If you are there in spring the primroses and other flowers will be a delight.

The path proceeds as a clear track, mercifully sloping gradually downwards through a wood (Whitehorse Wood) – better described, perhaps, as a coppice – for 900 m, coming out on a road. Turn right and in a short distance on the other side of the road, by the house, Poundgate, is the stile and footpath sign, the line of the path following the headland of the fields ahead of you, eventually passing between two lines of trees. After about 100 m, go through the iron gate on your left, turning right at once along the hedge, bringing you out on a road through another iron gate.

Turn right on the road passing Boughurst Street Farm on your right; then right, down the bridle-way signed 'to Wrangling Lane', fenced on the left; when the fencing ends, go straight on, following the field edge as far as the tall beech tree then descending diagonally to the far bottom corner of the field. A pleasant stretch of woodland path leads to the roadway where you turn right down the hill, passing the typical Kentish Buckland Farm on your left. The stile to the next part of the path will be seen on your left a few metres past a fork in the road.

In front of you lies the verdant valley known as Bowling Alley, a lovely panorama of wood and field. Go over the stile, and the next 1000 m of the Wealdway crosses the large field diagonally right to a stile in the wire fence. From the stile the line may not be clear but it continues in the same direction, skirting the edge of the patch of woodland on the slope ahead, making for the line of trees forming the field boundary and keeping to the left (east) of it. Go in between two gates and then down towards Luddesdown Church seen below, along the wire fence and over the stile. Bear right around the church wall.

For a description of Luddesdown see page 39. For refreshment and snacks (cheese rolls, etc.) the pub, The Golden Lion, is 500 m up the road going north.

Steps up the bank on the far side of the church gate and a stile lead
to the path along the field edge for 200 m. More steps on the right
lead down to the roadway; cross the road and carry straight on. Go
over a stile in the wire fence then left along the wire to another stile.
Turn right, climbing the steep slope; left along the line of
brushwood at the field edge, reaching a stile on your right. Cross
this stile and keep straight on up the slope. In 100 m a stile on the
left takes you through a narrow belt of trees and then down
alongside a line of trees, passing under a power line. At the bottom
of the slope there is a junction of paths; carry straight on ('FP 242',
Camer Park). The wide track winds past a very presentable 'cottage'
and finishes along the east fence of the Camer Country Park (page
36). Turn right on the road (B2009), past the Railway Inn and Sole
Street station. Meals and bar snacks are obtainable at the Railway
Inn daily including Sundays.

For descriptions of Sole Street village with the Yeoman's House,
and a diversion to Cobham*, see pages 36 and 53 and sketch map.

Over the railway, take the first turning on the left, Manor Road.
Join the signed path at the side of the last house on the left before
the bend in the road and almost immediately turn right at the
T-junction of paths, the route running along the bottom of
bungalow gardens. On reaching the road turn right and in a few
metres join the footpath on the left leading off a farm access track.
Go across the field to a stile in the wire fence, turning right and
keeping to the field edge before reaching a minor road (500 m).

Diversion to Nurstead* church (see page 61 and sketch map).

Cross the minor road, the path following the field boundary and
turning left at the corner of the field. Down a slight slope and over
two stiles you come to a stile by a field gate. Turn right along the
metalled access road passing some cottages in the hamlet of Nash
Street. Turn down the track on the right by Shepherd's Cottage and
follow it for 1½ miles (general direction north-east at first and then
north); you pass a large eighteenth-century farmhouse on the right,
Ifield Court.

Eventually an orchard is reached on the right of the path fringed by a row of small poplar trees. At the end of this row the Wealdway path leaves the track, crossing diagonally the large field on the left in the direction of the Tollgate Moat House, the roof of which can be seen to the north-west. Go through a gate in the Moat House fence, along a short length of path to the right and you have reached the last stile of the Wealdway.

Diversions

(a) *Cobham*. Walking mileage $3\frac{1}{2}$ miles (an extra $1\frac{1}{2}$ miles). Cobham is one of the most attractive villages in Kent. The fine church, whose present structure is 500 years old or more, with a magnificent collection of memorial brasses unmatched not only in Britain but in Europe; the New College behind the church (the 'new' refers to the sixteenth-century renovation!); links with powerful families of the Middle Ages and later whose splendid house sits in its noble parkland setting; links with Charles Dickens who as a boy lived in Chatham and came to love Cobham Park: all these contribute to Cobham's fascination.

Of the church, the large chancel was built in 1220 by Henry de Cobham on the site of an earlier church; the nave was added in 1362 by John de Cobham, a great benefactor who built at the same time the College behind the church to house priests to pray for his soul and those who came after. After the Dissolution William, Lord Cobham, enlarged the College in 1598 for the practical and charitable purpose of housing twenty poor pensioners. You can see these dwellings, equipped now with electricity and all modern conveniences, providing delightful homes set around a shining green courtyard. At the back, through the window you can glimpse the original fourteenth-century Hall, complete with its refectory table, now used as a meeting place for the occupants of the College.

The show-piece of the church is the collection of no fewer than nineteen magnificent brasses, most of them in the chancel, dating from 1299 to 1529. The excellent booklet obtainable in the church provides a description of each one and a translation of the inscriptions. The men are all clad in armour apart from four of the

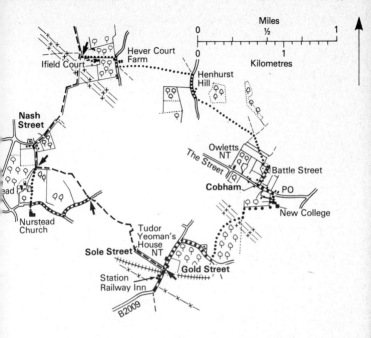

College's priests who are in their vestments. The ladies are most impressive; their dresses show that changing women's fashions are not a recent phenomenon!

The life-stories of some of those commemorated by these memorials excite interest. John de Cobham, for example, was at the height of his fortunes in 1362 at the time he built the nave and founded the College: prominent at the Court of Richard II he was accused of implication in a plot against his master and was banished to Jersey. He was then 80 but was eventually freed and died in 1407, when he must have been nearly 100. You can also see the brass of his wife, Margaret.

The Street, Cobham, and Leather Bottle Inn

Lady Joan de Cobham (1433), shown with her six sons and four daughters, must have had a life full of incident. She had five husbands; one wonders if it were her beauty or her possessions that attracted – probably both as she would presumably have inherited the estates of those who had 'gone before'. All appear to have been worthy knights but it is the marriage to her fourth husband, Sir John

The New College, Cobham, with church tower beyond

Oldcastle, that stirs my imagination the most. What strains this union must have had to bear! Sir John was an outstanding figure of the age. Born in the Welsh border.country, and a close friend of the young Prince Henry, later Henry V, he was the 'Falstaff' of Shakespeare's *Henry IV*. A brave soldier and apparently of an independent disposition, he became later in life a Lollard, supporting John Wycliffe's ideas for reform, protesting against many church practices and doctrines. Condemned as a heretic, he escaped from the Tower of London, taking refuge for four years in his native Welsh hills, hidden by his friends. Eventually captured he was 'hung and burnt' in London's Smithfield in 1417, thus becoming one of England's first Protestant martyrs of rank. One wonders what Lady Joan thought of her husband's cruel fate. Perhaps she, too, was a Lollard at heart. At the time it was said that every other person was a secret Lollard. Many years later, after the Protestant King James I came to the throne, Shakespeare – having incurred disapproval for grossly caricaturing the real Sir John Oldcastle's character – was forced to change the 'Sir John Oldcastle' appearing in the first editions of *Henry IV* to 'Sir John Falstaff'.

Lady Joan had one more husband, Sir John Harpendon, who survived her death in 1433. Of her ten children only one, a daughter, was living at her death and she inherited the estate.

William, Lord Cobham, who rebuilt the New College behind the church, was Lord Chamberlain at the court of Queen Elizabeth and one of her favourites. She is said to have visited Cobham twice during her life but when James I succeeded her his fortunes took a dive. He was caught up in the trumped-up treason charge James laid against Sir Walter Raleigh, William's friend. Raleigh was executed in 1616 but William suffered an almost equal ordeal: he was pardoned on the scaffold. When the Civil War broke out he, understandably, fought on the side of Parliament and was killed in the battle of Newbury.

Opposite the church is the Leather Bottle Inn known the world over for its association with Charles Dickens. Dickens lived in Chatham as a boy and must have known Cobham from his earliest days. In 1857 when he was rich and famous he came to live at Gad's Hill, less than a mile north of Cobham Park. Readers of *Pickwick Papers* will remember how Mr Pickwick and his friends from the Pickwick Club walked from Rochester to Cobham through the 'long vistas of stately oaks' of the park to rescue the impressionable Mr Tupman who, suffering from a thwarted love affair, had cut himself off (very comfortably) from the world to nurse his wounds at the Leather Bottle. Dickens enthusiasts will also recall that, having persuaded Tupman to rejoin the Club, Samuel Pickwick, on leaving the inn, discovered in the street outside a stone with a mysterious inscription, and that the learned paper he subsequently wrote on the subject of this antiquity earned him acclaim in scientific circles and honorary membership of no fewer than seventeen societies at home and abroad! Nor was his reputation much affected when some rival pointed out that the words could be interpreted to read 'BILL STUMPS HIS MARK'. If you want to try your skill at deciphering you can do so as you will find the controversial stone itself by the outside wall of the Leather Bottle on the street corner!

One mile north-east of Cobham, with the entrance just off the B2009 (Cobham's 'The Street'), is Cobham Hall, site of the homes of the de Cobhams and their successors over the centuries. The unfortunate William, Lord Cobham mentioned above started to build the present impressive mansion in the early 1600s but the forefeiture of his estates after the treason charge postponed completion for half-a-century. Nevertheless the Hall is a magnificent example of late Elizabethan architecture, with later additions. The Hall is now a school but the gardens can be visited daily on certain dates in the school Easter and summer holidays.

The park is crossed by public footpaths (you can see a map in Cobham village opposite the school). There is a curious mausoleum built by one of the Bligh family, Lords of Cobham in the eighteenth century. It was never used and is now much vandalised.

The park was the scene of tragedy in the extraordinary story of the talented Kentish Victorian painter, Richard Dadd, born in Chatham. Dadd's earliest sketches were of Cobham Park and as a youngster he was a frequent visitor to the Hall, where he was able to see the fine collection of paintings. He continued to show great promise after he moved with his parents to London, where he joined a group of up-and-coming young artists. After a tour of the Continent, Turkey and Egypt with some of the group he began to show signs of insanity. One day in 1843 he suggested to his father that they should spend a few days in the country; they travelled down to Cobham and after a meal at the Ship Inn found lodgings in the village. Richard then proposed a walk in Cobham Park, which they both knew and loved. Once in the park he stabbed his father to death. Fleeing to Dover he crossed to France, taking the diligence going south. He told a fellow traveller he was going to kill the Pope and then tried to strangle him. Arrested by the police he was eventually returned to London, where he was tried and sentenced to detention in an asylum for the rest of his life. First in Royal Bedlam and then in the newly-opened Broadmoor, Dadd continued to produce an astonishing series of imaginative paintings right up to his death in 1883. Exhibitions of his works in recent years have aroused considerable interest and in 1982 one of his works fetched £500,000 at a sale. A hollow in the park, which can be seen from the road 400 m from Cobham village, is known as 'Dadd's Hole'.

You can get food and refreshment daily in Cobham's three inns: the Leather Bottle, the Ship and the Darnley Arms. Light meals and teas can also be had at Smith's the Bakers in The Street. There is a Post Office and a fifteenth-century grocery store!

Directions for southbound walkers
On reaching the first kink in the path approaching Ifield Court (page 32) turn sharp left on the metalled farm track passing in front of Ifield Court. On reaching the roadway turn right keeping the white wooden fence of Hever Court Farm on your left. Take the footpath on the left (indicated by a signpost) that runs along the east fence of the farm. The path breasts the slope ahead crossing a farm track at right angles and continuing in the same direction (now also a farm track). A gate is reached giving on to the roadway; turn right down the hill (Henhurst Hill) passing a few houses on the right. You will see the footpath on the left by the side of the last cottage (there is a signpost about 15 m in from the road). The line of the path should be clear up the slope in front of you, continuing as a farm track near the crest of the slope. Carry on past a rubbish pit on your left to a holly tree seen ahead. From here a narrower path takes you to the corner of the field ahead and the exit on to a country lane. Turn right down the lane (you will see on the right fine examples of 'desirable residences' converted from five oast houses) and in 300 m turn left on the main road, the B2009, for the short distance to Cobham.

By turning right instead of left on the B2009 you come (in 200 m) to a National Trust property, Owletts, a fine country residence built in the reign of Charles II and restored by the architect, Sir Herbert Baker, who lived there and gave the house to the Trust. It has a staircase and ceiling which are particularly fine. It is open to the public from April to September from 2–5 p.m. on Wednesdays and Thursdays.

To rejoin the Wealdway after visiting Cobham join the footpath leading up some steps from The Street (the main road) opposite the Leather Bottle. This path leads through the churchyard skirting the church and along the west side of the New College. Cross the stile on the right bringing you through the small cemetery. On leaving the cemetery follow the track along the edge of the field and the line of poplars. At the end of the line of poplars turn left; the track will bring you, in 150 m, at the corner of an orchard fringed by poplars, to a path on the right, following the line of poplars sheltering the orchard. Keep to the line of poplars when the path bears left and you will emerge on a road. Turn right and, passing a large house, Danes Place, on the right, after 800 m you reach the junction with the main B2009 road. Turn left, and a short walk (passing the Yeoman's House on the right – see page 36) will bring you to Sole Street railway bridge and the Wealdway (page 36).

Directions for northbound walkers
Instead of turning left down Manor Road, Sole Street, after crossing the railway bridge (page 51), keep straight on the main road, the B2009, for 500 m and take the first turning on the right, Gold Street – there is a white house on the corner. Walk down the road, past a large house, Danes Place, and in 250 m on the left will be seen a concrete sign indicating a footpath that follows a line of poplars sheltering an orchard – there are also yellow waymarks painted on posts along the path. Follow the path as it curves to the right, still following the poplars. At the end of the orchard the path reaches a farm track – the tower of Cobham church should be visible among the trees to the north. Turn left (north) on the farm track and when it joins an east-west track fringing a line of poplars, turn right. You

come to a stile and a 'squeeze' gate fringing a cemetery. Keep on, turning left at the far side of the cemetery, the path bringing you alongside the New College and to the church porch. The main road (B2009), known as The Street, is ahead of you.

To rejoin the Wealdway proceed westwards down The Street. You pass the old village pump given by the Darnleys early last century, and then to a turning on the right, Battle Street. Take this lane – there is a striking 'residential development' incorporating no fewer than five oast houses *en route*.

If you continue along The Street, past the Battle Street turning, you come after 200 m to a National Trust property, Owletts (see page 59).

300 m down Battle Street, past the last house on the left, an opening in the hedge gives on to a large field with a footpath crossing diagonally towards a solitary holly tree. From there the route continues on a wide track, eventually after 600 m descending to a minor road by some cottages. Turn right up the hill (Henshurst Hill), passing a few houses on the left. At the top of the slope, where the power-line crosses the road, there is on the left a gate to a wide track. Through this gate, your path leads along the track for 900 m to the roadway, the last few metres alongside the white wooden fence of a newly built farm, Hever Court Farm. Turn right past this farm, then take the first on the left on a private metalled road with a post-box. Carry straight on, passing in front of Ifield Court, an impressive eighteenth-century country house with a fifteenth-century flint structure at the back. For the final section of the Wealdway, turn right at the solitary chestnut tree on the right of the metalled track.

(b) *Nurstead Church*. Walking mileage ¾ mile (an extra ¼ mile). Nurstead church, standing out prominently in the landscape, goes back to the fourteenth and fifteenth centuries but was built on the site of a much earlier one. A church at 'Nutstede' is mentioned in the Domesday Book (1086) and could probably have been of Saxon origin. Of interest are the memorials to the Edmeades family who have lived at Nurstead Court for generations and who are still there. The Court, barely visible among the trees 100 m or so north of the church, is unique in that part of the Great Hall erected in the fourteenth century with lofty supporting timbers still survives, matched in Britain by only one or two others for its antiquity and state of preservation. Unfortunately it is not possible to visit the Court.

Directions for southbound walkers
After turning left down the metalled farm access road at Nash Street (see sketch map), instead of turning left over the stile by the field gate (the Wealdway), proceed through or over the gate itself. Although this is marked 'Private' there is a right-of-way straight ahead towards the church across the field. The line runs alongside the wall of the Nurstead Court estate and comes out by the right-hand side of the lodge on the road, opposite the church. In wet weather the path is a quagmire; as an alternative, proceed on the Wealdway from Nash Street until the path crosses a roadway. Turn right and, keeping right at the fork, you reach Nurstead church in about ten minutes (see sketch map).

      After visiting the church, turn left down the road, left at the fork and rejoin the Wealdway where it crosses the roadway.

Directions for northbound walkers
Where the Wealdway crosses a roadway about 800 m from Manor Road in Sole Street (see sketch map), turn left down the road and you reach the church in 700 m. To rejoin the Wealdway, turn right out of the church gate and you will see a concrete footpath sign by the side of the lodge opposite. The path runs at the side of the lodge and in a straight line, through a farm gate and along the wall of the Nurstead Court estate. Keep on across the field to a wooden field gate; go over or through this and you are back on the Wealdway at Nash Street. In wet conditions the Nurstead path is a quagmire; as an alternative, return from the church by the road, the way you came.

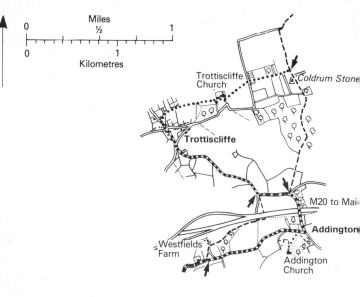

Miles
0   ½   1

Kilometres
0   1

Trottiscliffe
Church

Coldrum Stone

Trottiscliffe

M20 to Mai

Addington

Westfields
Farm

Addington
Church

(c) *Trottiscliffe*. Walking mileage 1¾ miles (an extra ½ mile).
The first thing that should be known about Trottiscliffe is that it is
pronounced 'Trosley'. If anyone reading this guide is a stranger to
Britain and wants to know why the spelling of the village's name is
ignored when it is spoken one can only say 'Don't know'. If one asks
the villagers themselves they would probably say 'Why shouldn't
we?'

Anyhow, it is a pleasant place to break off for a rest and
refreshment. You come to the church first, some way from the
village, probably indicating that an earlier village covered a much
greater area. Apart from the ravages of the Black Death there has
been a steady depopulation of the countryside over the last
centuries. The first mention of the village and church is in Saxon

Trottiscliffe Church and North Downs

times, 788 AD, and the description of the building you will find in the church pinpoints where you can trace Saxon features although the main structure is Norman. There are some bones exhibited from the Long Barrow of Coldrum and brasses of a fifteenth-century lawyer and his wife. Next to the church is the elegant eighteenth-century Court Lodge and a farm. The village itself,

800 m further on, has all the qualities of a charming Kent village:
warm red brick houses behind high walls, a trim village pond and
borders of sweet-smelling flowers. It is a quiet backwater where you
can sit outside either of the two fifteenth-century pubs, the Plough
and the George, and enjoy it.

Directions for southbound walkers
On approaching the prominent National Trust Coldrum site and
about 100 m from it, the stile and footpath sign to Trottiscliffe will
be seen on the right. After passing through a housing estate and
over the road, the path continues, dipping down to the wooden
hollow where Trottiscliffe church and Court Lodge lie. Passing in
front of the lodge and the farm beside it, the path – now a farm track
– carries on to the village of Trottiscliffe with some fine views of the
Downs on the right. After some pleasant houses – one of them,
Long Gore House, is over 400 years old – you reach the roadway.
Turn left, and the two pubs, the Plough and the George, and the
Post Office Stores are only a few metres beyond the village pond.
To rejoin the Wealdway, go over the crossroads and follow the road
signed 'Addington, W. Malling' for ¾ mile. On the right, by the fence
of the large quarry workings, 'Olley (Wrotham) Ltd', is the stile and
waymark of the Wealdway going south under the M20 motorway
(page 47).

Directions for northbound walkers
After passing under the M20 motorway and continuing the few
metres to the road (page 49), turn *left* – instead of right for the
Wealdway – and in ¾ mile you reach Trottiscliffe with its two pubs,
the George and the Plough, Post Office Stores and village pond. To
rejoin the Wealdway, continue straight on north through the village
until, on the outskirts, on the right will be seen Green Lane. This
leads past the sixteenth-century Long Gore House, to the track to
Court Lodge and Trottiscliffe church and then over a roadway,
through an estate and by a footpath to the Wealdway, just north of
the National Trust Coldrum Long Barrow site.

Note: The Post Office Stores in Trottiscliffe is open only in the mornings and until 1.45 p.m. except on Fridays and Saturdays when it is open all day up to 4.30 p.m. At both the Plough and the George pubs you can get something to eat at lunchtime and in the evenings every day including Saturdays and Sundays, a welcome facility.

(d) *Addington*. Walking mileage 1 mile (same distance as Wealdway route).

Although the M20 runs only a few metres away, Addington (Old English 'Eadda's farm') seems to be little affected – the deep cutting of the motorway deadens the sound, leaving it an enviable backwater: a village green with two oak trees provides a perfect setting for a cluster of cottages, Post Office Stores and the fourteenth-century Angel Inn.

At first sight Addington is a normal charming village, but within a short distance from the village green there are traces of human settlement 7000 or more years ago. 400 m along the country road, Park Road, opposite the green and just past the small estate, The Chestnuts, on the right, a group of huge sarsen stones will be seen in a field right by the road. These are the remains of a Neolithic chamber tomb (about 3000 BC) similar to the Coldrum Long Barrow at Trottiscliffe. The site has been excavated a number of times and traces of nine burials found. Mesolithic (Mid-Stone Age: 4000 BC or earlier) flint implements were also discovered. The objects found are in the Maidstone Museum.

Addington's fifteenth-century church lies in Addington Park: follow the drive leading off Park Road on the left near the village green. The church is apparently built on an artificial mound, possibly an early defensive site – churches often had a dual role. No date is suggested but the site could go back to the Dark Ages or even pre-Roman days. The church appears to be open only when a service takes place.

Addington Post Office Stores is open until 5.30 p.m. on weekdays (early closing Thursday and Saturday, 1 p.m.). The Angel pub serves lunches and bar snacks every day except Sunday.

Directions for southbound walkers

Coming down from the Coldrum site (page 43) take the road on
the *left* at the T-junction, leading over the M20 motorway. Once
over the bridge you come in 500 m to the village green at
Addington. To rejoin the Wealdway you can either retrace your
steps across the motorway, turning left at the T-junction beyond the
bridge, or follow Park Road, a pleasant country road starting
opposite the village green. This will take you past the chamber tomb
mentioned above. You continue along the road until it dips down to
a brick bridge over a stream (1¼ miles). For the Wealdway turn right
on the footpath a few metres up the slope beyond the bridge (page
48).

Directions for northbound walkers

Instead of turning left on the footpath by the bungalow Southfields
(page 49), continue straight on along the road. This will bring you
(800 m) to the village green in Addington. As you approach the
village, on your left in a field by the roadside and immediately
before a small housing estate, are the remains of a Neolithic
chamber tomb noted above.

To rejoin the Wealdway, take the road north from the village
green; this crosses the M20 motorway by a bridge. Turn right at the
T-junction beyond the bridge and you are back on the Wealdway
(see sketch map).

Public transport

Gravesend

Passenger ferry Gravesend (West Pier)–Tilbury (Riverside). Daily.
    Half-hourly service, more frequent at peak hours. Crossing five
    minutes.
British Rail Frequent daily services: London (Charing Cross)–
    Dartford–*Gravesend*–Chatham–Gillingham.
Green Line Coach services 725/6. (Windsor) W. Croydon–
    Bromley–Dartford–*Gravesend*. Weekdays, hourly; Sundays,
    two-hourly.

Bus services From and to Gravesend BR station. Most bus services
connect with trains to and from London. Tollgate Moat House
(A2), start of Wealdway: MD 308/9, 314/5/6. Weekdays,
frequent; Sundays, hourly. Sole Street: MD 310. Weekdays only,
infrequent. Alternative: Meopham (Parade), 1 mile from Sole
Street: MD 308/9, 314/5/6. Weekdays, half-hourly; Sundays,
two-hourly. Wrotham Heath: MD 308/9. Gravesend–Meopham
BR–Borough Green–*Wrotham Heath*. Weekdays, hourly;
Sundays, two-hourly.

Sole Street

British Rail Daily services: London (Victoria)–Bromley S.–*Sole
Street*–Chatham–Gillingham. Weekdays, half-hourly, Sundays,
hourly.
Bus services Gravesend: MD 310. Weekdays only, infrequent.
Alternative: Meopham (Parade), 1 mile from Sole Street. MD
308/9, 314/5/6. Weekdays, half-hourly; Sundays, two-hourly.

Wrotham Heath

Bus services Borough Green BR: Weekdays, frequent services;
Sundays, approx. two-hourly. Gravesend–Meopham BR–
Borough Green–*Wrotham Heath*–W. Malling BR–Maidstone:
MD 10, 308. Weekdays, hourly; Sundays, two-hourly.

Note MD = Maidstone & District. Service enquiries: telephone
Borough Green (0732) 882128.

Accommodation

Gravesend

Mrs E. B. Haynes Sunnyside Guest House Windmill Street Gravesend DA12 1LG Telephone Gravesend (0474) 65445	B&B. Evening meal if advised in advance.	7 minutes' walk from town centre towards A2.

Addington

Mrs E. Smart Westfields Farm Addington West Malling Kent ME19 5BW Telephone West Malling (0732) 843209	B&B.	Right on route.

Wrotham Heath

Fredericks Hotel (formerly White Rose) London Road Wrotham Heath Sevenoaks Kent TN15 7RX Telephone Borough Green (0732) 884149	B&B. Evening meal except Sundays.	On route.

Section 2

Wrotham Heath to **Tonbridge** 14 miles

General description

As is to be expected, on most of the Wealdway – over 50 miles of
the total 80 miles – you will be walking over that expanse, most of it
former forest, the Weald, and it is on this section that you first
encounter some of the characteristic 'Wealden' features.

The sand quarries of Addington at the end of the previous section
are evidence that you have left behind the chalk of the North
Downs country and are on the clay or sandy soil of the Weald. As
mentioned in the chapter on background, from ancient times
settlements in the Weald have been more scattered than in most of
southern England as the nature of much of the soil has not been
suitable for crops or pasture (except for pigs) so, in contrast to the
Gravesend to Wrotham Heath section, where you had villages every
few miles with a pub for rest and refreshment, here such anemities
are rarer. On the whole 14 miles you have the Blue Anchor at Platt
(only 1½ miles from Wrotham Heath), the Swan at charming West
Peckham and the Bell Inn at Golden Green. Unless you have food
with you it is advisable to time your stops to coincide with 'opening
time'. There are, of course, good facilities for refreshment and
accommodation at Wrotham Heath and Tonbridge.

The Weald is mostly upland with a few low-lying sandy and more
fertile areas carved out by the rivers, and on this section you
traverse both types of country. After leaving Wrotham Heath you
pass at first through some pleasant woods and conifer plantations,
the latter resplendent in late spring with rhododendrons,
characteristic of the clay soils, and then through part of the hamlet
of Platt with some well-designed modern homes, many converted
from old village dwellings, before beginning the gradual climb of the
Weald where the path runs for 2 miles along the western edge of
Mereworth Woods (pronounced 'Merryworth').

Looking at the map you would be excused for imagining you have before you a leafy paradise of noble trees but this is a true 'Wealden' expanse: the woods are a large area of almost 6 square miles which, apart from a few patches, has been denuded of its trees over the centuries. Much of Mereworth Woods is coppice – where the sprouts from stumps of trees, mostly hazel and ash, are cut and used for fencing, etc. This leaves the landscape somewhat bare but you occasionally come across a few loftly single beeches or oaks standing out on the scene like giant signposts – which they probably are. The Wealdway rises gradually from 100 to 170 m (330 to 560 ft) to the edge of the escarpment at Gover Hill, a National Trust area, with the southern slope dipping steeply down to the valley of the river Medway (Old English 'sweet water'). From Gover Hill, particularly when the trees are bare of leaves, there is a fine view of the broad valley with its pastures, orchards and hop-gardens.

After dropping down from the hill the path continues to present most attractive views of the country ahead of you. There is then a dull stretch of flat fields apt to be muddy in wet conditions before the path crosses a vast orchard that in springtime provides one of the unforgettable sights of the Wealdway: miles and miles of blossoming fruit trees. On this part of the path in April I have stopped to marvel at apple blossom as far as I could see: on either side, before and behind me. A short distance further on, past the hamlet of Barnes Street, you come to the Medway.

The originators of the Wealdway have done a great service by routing 4 miles of the path along the river. You walk along the banks of the Medway for over an hour with hardly a building in sight for the whole distance until you approach Tonbridge and, given reasonable weather, there could hardly be a more pleasant walk in the country, through rich pastures and woods with a profusion of wild flowers and, in the spring, an unceasing chorus of bird song.

The approach to Tonbridge is hardly impressive, sheds and workshops almost crowding you off the path, but once you reach the centre of the town the thirteenth-century castle surrounded by beautiful gardens and the half-timbered houses of the High Street soon restore morale.

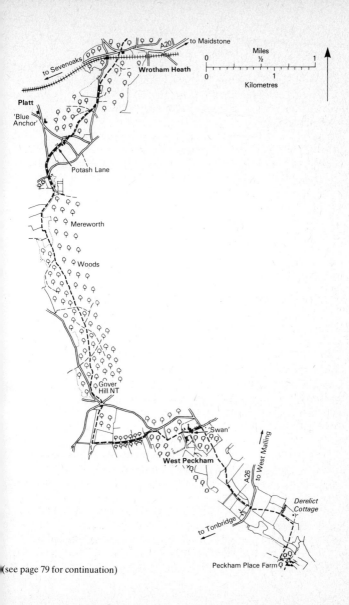

(see page 79 for continuation)

One other delightful feature of the Weald is the use of the warm, honey-coloured sandstone in the construction of its ancient buildings. Tonbridge Castle, Tonbridge church and Barnes Place at Barnes Street are all examples, spanning nearly 800 years, to be seen on the path.

This second section of the Wealdway is not tiring and there are no steep gradients. Northbound walkers have the slope of Gover Hill to climb but this is quite short. Wet conditions could leave the low-lying parts of the walk rather muddy.

MAPS
OS 1:50 000 188
OS 1:25 000 TQ 65/75, 64/74, 44/54

Route Southbound

Almost opposite the spot where the Wealdway emerges on to the A20 at Wrotham Heath is the Fredericks (formerly the White Rose) Hotel. Alongside the hotel is the wide entry to a bridle-way – the continuation of the Wealdway. There is an official blue bridle-way sign as well as the Wealdway waymark. In a few metres you pass under a railway bridge and a little farther on, where the path branches, take the right-hand fork. The path starts to rise gently through some pleasant woodland and after about 500 m from the railway bridge you eventually reach a country road. Turn left on the road and, passing Valley Cottage on your left, you enter a world of tall conifers, rhododendron clumps and opulent houses. The Wealdway continues as a narrow path on the right between hurdle fences just after passing the drive marked 'Wingate' (concrete footpath sign and waymark). The path slopes gently down through the conifers and rhododendrons; keep the same direction where there are paths crossing at right angles. At the bottom of the descent there is a white house, Rough Acres, on your left; the path continues between high hedges bordering the garden, bringing you out on a narrow roadway. Turn right and take the turning on the left, Potash Lane.

This lies on the outskirts of the hamlet of Platt (the name is a

Platt village

variation of 'plot'; in fact, on a sixteenth-century map of properties in the area that hangs in the lounge of the Blue Anchor Inn, you will see the centre of the village is marked 'Plotte'). If, instead of turning up Potash Lane, you carry straight on you come to the nineteenth-century church of St Mary the Virgin, some interesting little cottages on the north side and, a few steps farther on, the comfortable Blue Anchor inn opposite, converted from a sixteenth-century house and barn (meals and snacks Mondays to Fridays; snacks on Saturdays and Sundays at midday). There is also a Post Office Stores open daily except Thursday afternoons and Sundays.

To rejoin the Wealdway turn right out of the pub and follow the right-hand fork; after 500 m the road is joined on the left by Potash Lane. This is the Wealdway.

Potash Lane is lined on each side by attractive modern houses, some converted from older village buildings: one is dated 1637. Go straight ahead where Potash Lane joins a road coming in on the right by the neat Kettle Cottage and over the crossroads, passing Napps Farm on your left. 200 m down the road junction you will see on your right two concrete bridle-way signs: take the right hand one – it could be a bit muddy at the start in wet weather.

For the next 2 miles you will be following this track along the western boundary of the vast Mereworth Woods, a sparse Wealden coppice area. Apart from a waymark at a junction of paths 700 m from the start there is no sign to guide you, but the way is not difficult to follow if you keep straight on in a south-easterly direction along the wide track. From time to time you have a glimpse of extensive views on the right. The path gradually rises until you come to Gover Hill (170 m–560 ft) (National Trust) on the edge of the escarpment. Here you have some fine views of the Medway valley ahead of you, some of the most fertile lands of the Weald.

After descending Gover Hill, the Wealdway continues by the well-marked bridle-way starting by the left-hand (east) side of the white cottage at the road junction below the hill. This slopes pleasantly down affording some lovely views on all sides as you make your way. Turn left at the end of the fencing (waymarked), the path running along the south headland (boundary) of the field. At the field edge you turn right into the wide unmetalled farm track between a double avenue of splendid beech trees. Turn left on the roadway where the track ends by a lodge.

View looking south-west from Gover Hill

A footpath will be seen leading off the roadway on the right by some white painted railings. Follow this path, which bends to the right along the boundary of an orchard. Opposite the farm bungalow turn left along the southern boundary of the orchard; go through the kissing-gate and diagonally across the charming village green (unless there is a cricket match going on!).

The Wealdway looking south from Gover Hill

West Peckham (Old English 'village near the hill'), one of the Weald's most attractive villages, is of ancient origin. Although it appears in the Domesday Book as supporting 25 serfs and their families there is no mention of the church although this certainly has definite Saxon features both in the tower and the nave. The church and the village green with its venerable trees make a perfect picture and in fine weather you can sit outside the Swan Inn, winner of a prize for the best country pub, and bask in its beauty. Inside the church there is a former chantry on the north side of the chancel which has been converted into a curious family pew for the squire. The chantry was built in the early fifteenth century by Sir John Colepepper, one of Henry IV's judges, for prayers to be said for his and the king's soul. It was suppressed at the Dissolution in 1548, and a more utilitarian purpose found for it. A sixteenth-century house down the road, Duke's Place, incorporates what remains of a house of the Knights Hospitallers of St John of Jerusalem, an Order originating in the Crusades of which our well-known nursing Order of St John's is the successor. This house was founded in 1408 by the same Sir John Colepepper. A note in the informative booklet you can find in the church tells us the members were unfailing in their care for the poor and needy of the locality. Duke's Place is not open to the public. The Swan Inn serves meals daily including Sundays. The Post Office is open 8.30 a.m.–12.30 p.m. Mondays to Fridays. Only soft drinks are sold – no groceries.

For the next section of the Wealdway continue eastwards down the village's main street; after a short distance there is a road (signposted 'Hadlow, Tonbridge') on the left. Opposite this turning is the path, indicated by a concrete footpath sign and a waymark. At first the path is narrow and between fences; after crossing a stile go straight ahead to a field gate. From this gate the line of the path is towards a tree in front of you marked with a white 'blob' painted on the trunk. By this tree is a waymarked stile. From this stile make diagonally for the corner of the next field. Go over the stile in the corner and the line of the path follows the ditch on your right hand and you eventually emerge on the main road, the A26.

Cross the road and just to the right there is a concrete footpath sign and waymark by a gate. From the gate the line of the path runs almost due east, i.e. diagonally to the left across the field. As a guide you can make for the right-hand tree of the line of trees seen on the far field boundary. By this tree is a stile and waymark: after crossing the stile go straight on, keeping the derelict cottage about 50 m on your left, to a stile in a wire fence. Turn sharp right after this stile to a copse with two small streams. Go through two gates, over the two footbridges and on to the track, passing two disused corrugated iron huts. Turn left at the junction of paths (there is a hop-garden on your right) on to a metalled farm track that bends to the right past the buildings of Peckham Place Farm and leads to the road.

Turn left on the road and in 100 m turn right, over the stile with a footpath sign and waymark indicating the path running along the side of the lofty corrugated iron barns of Crowhurst Farm in a south-westerly direction through an extensive orchard covering several acres. It is this stretch of the Wealdway that provides sensational vistas in springtime of apple blossom on either side of the path. The route runs straight as a die through countless trees with here and there a beehive placed strategically to extract as much honey as possible from the flowers.

For just under a mile the path runs straight, crossing a footbridge over the flat lands of the valley. On reaching a roadway, turn right making for a most impressive residential complex, Kent House Place, formed from no fewer than six oast houses. The road runs between this and Kent House Farm. Turn left down the very narrow lane (keep an eye open for any cars) that brings you to Pierce Mill, turned into two flats, on the right. Here the path turns off to the right and follows the north bank of the stream, the Bourne river, that meanders its way down to the Medway from higher ground not far from Platt, north of Mereworth Woods. After 400 m cross the footbridge, then two more footbridges into the next field and in a few metres to the roadway.

Turn right on the road; opposite is Barnes Place, an imposing timbered house parts of which are 600 years old (no visiting facilities). Continue along the road for a few steps and the path (indicated by a concrete footpath sign) will be seen on the left just past the garden of Barnes Place. Go over the stile and, turning left along the wire fence, passing behind the farm buildings, cross the stile with a footpath sign and waymark on your right. This takes you straight on by the side of a draining ditch on your left and an orchard on your right. This orchard, too, is a picture in blossom time, with sheep grazing beneath the trees, so keep your camera ready.

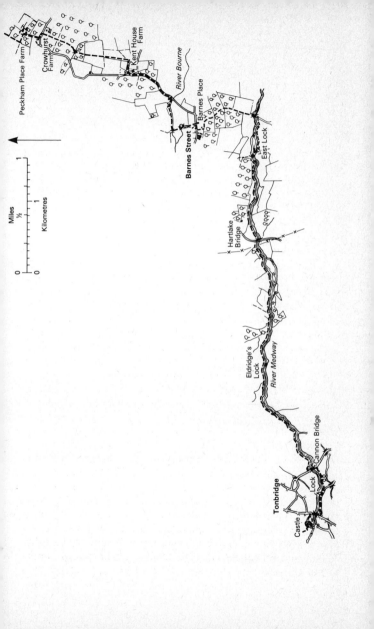

Peckham Place Farm

Crowhurst Farm

Kent House Farm

River Bourne

Barnes Place

Barnes Street

East Lock

Hartlake Bridge

Eldridge's Lock

River Medway

Tonbridge

Lock

Cannon Bridge

Castle

Miles
0   ½   1
0   1
Kilometres

Blossom at West Peckham

If in need of refreshment, and it is opening time, you will find the Bell Inn by continuing straight on for ¾ mile beyond Barnes Place to the straggling village of Golden Green, made unattractive by light industrial plants along the road. The Bell serves meals during the week and snacks on Saturdays and Sundays. There is also a Post Office Stores open daily except Thursday afternoon and Sunday.

Oast House, Crowhurst Farm

The path bordering the orchard brings you through two gates to a magnificent new iron footbridge over the Medway. The bridge itself is a good place to linger and gaze over the quiet waters of the river, here about 30 m across. You have in front of you 4 miles of splendid riverside walking, three locks and a road bridge the only man-made feature on the whole stretch.

The Wealdway at Barnes Street

As you come off the iron footbridge turn right. Although there is no clear track the line of the path closely follows the south bank of the river through the meadow grass until the first lock (East Lock) is reached. Cross the river by this lock and turn left over the two footbridges. The path continues from here on the north bank all the way to Tonbridge.

The Medway near East Lock

Those interested will delight in the variety of birds and bird-song in spring and early summer. Apart from the water birds, mallard, coot, moorhen and so on, there are willow warblers, chiffchaff and blackcap filling the woods with song, and reed warblers churring away in the reeds. There are also wild flowers in profusion. I found the comfrey particularly interesting, having learned that this tall

The Medway, Porter's Lock

hairy plant with mauve flowers which grows in damp places by the river bank is rich in protein, yielding twenty times as much as soya beans. Research is taking place on its wider use as animal or possibly human nutrient.

Between East Lock and the next lock on the path you may notice what looks like an old milestone by the footpath. This is a reminder that in the early eighteenth century a lot of work was done on this part of the river to make it navigable as far as Tonbridge. Timber and hops were shipped to Rochester, Chatham and beyond and chalk and lime for building brought back to Tonbridge. The coming of the railway in 1842 brought about a gradual decline in the use of the river but it is fine for pleasure boats: you may see a long boat or two making its leisurely way.

The one road bridge you pass under, Hartlake Bridge, was the scene of a tragic accident in October 1853. Two wagon-loads of hop-pickers, men, women and children, were being driven back to their camp after work. When crossing the bridge, then a flimsy wooden affair, a leading horse stumbled, broke the rail and fell into the river. Both wagons were tipped into the water and the 35 hop-pickers, all from the East End of London, were drowned. There is a memorial to them in Hadlow church.

The approach to Tonbridge by the river path is hardly attractive but you can penetrate into the heart of the town. Keep on the path, past some industrial buildings, until it brings you on to the road bridge, Cannon Bridge. Cross to the other side of the bridge, bear left and join the footpath now running along the south bank of the river. You unfortunately cannot avoid the gas holders but the basin of the Town Lock is pleasant enough: you come out on Medway Wharf Road. A few metres more and you reach Tonbridge's High Street and the Big Bridge over the Medway. The magnificent ruin of Tonbridge's castle you will see to your left over the bridge.

Tonbridge (Old English 'Dun Burgh', Hillfort, perhaps referring to the Iron Age castle hill fort 2 miles south-east).
Tonbridge sprang up around its castle, built to defend the Medway crossing on the route from London to Rye and Hastings, one of the most important in southern England. There may have been a stronghold here in Saxon times but the Normans wasted no time after the Conquest in erecting one of their formidable castles. At first a wooden fortification on a huge artificial mound, soon followed by stone structures, the present castle was built in the

Town Lock, Tonbridge

early thirteenth century after previous ones had been burnt down –
the owners more than once incurring royal wrath and suffering
sieges. Curiously enough, the castle is not mentioned in the
Domesday Book although it must have been there in 1086.
'Richard de Tonbridge', a kinsman of the Conquerer's, is
mentioned several times in Domesday as the holder of Kentish

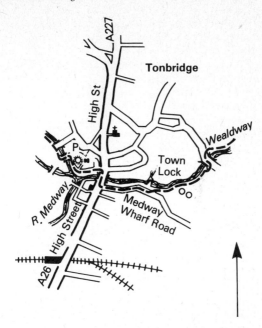

manors. The massive walls of the fortified area on the south side along the river still remain and can be admired from the River Walk. Only a small part of the central keep remains; the moat that surrounded the main area is now a green lawn where children play. Overlooking the lawns is the well-preserved gatehouse, one of the finest in the country. In addition to the usual defences, portcullis, drawbridge and so on, on the top level there is a fine residential hall.

The castle was involved in many of the disputes in the Middle Ages. It was the stronghold of the powerful de Clare family, one of whom was a signatory of the Magna Carta; later King John seized the castle in revenge. It was temporarily the Royal Court in the thirteenth century when the Prince of Wales (later Edward II) was acting for his father, Edward I, during his absence abroad. Although during the Civil War Tonbridge declared for Parliament, the owner of the castle at that time was a Royalist and the defences were destroyed, much of the stone being removed by the local residents of the town.

Other historic buildings in Tonbridge are the sixteenth-century Chequers Inn in the High Street and the shop next door of the same period. The origin of the hangman's noose on the Chequers signboard seems a mystery: perhaps it was a warning in the old days of what could happen to you if you missed paying your bill! In East Street there is the house of the Portreeve or customs officer. In Bordyke – part of the mediaeval ramparts – is the Priory, a large house, parts of which are all that remain of an Augustinian priory suppressed under Henry VIII who, however, may be credited for building the Great Bridge for the town, predecessor of the present one.

The large parish church of Tonbridge tucked away behind the High Street is of Norman origin, the north aisle being thirteenth-century but the rest mainly a Victorian restoration. The impressive buildings of Tonbridge School, the famous public school are at the north end of the High Street.

The castle can be visited, 11.30 a.m.–1.00 p.m. and 2.00–5.30 p.m. 30 April–29 May and 4 June–24 July weekends only; 25 July–11September daily.

Route Northbound
Turn right (south) over the Big Bridge in Tonbridge High Street and take the first turning on the left, Medway Wharf Road, bearing left off the road by the lock (the Town Lock) and following the asphalted riverside path past the gas holders. On reaching the road bridge, Cannon Bridge, turn left on the roadway and cross over, down to the footpath that follows the north bank of the river.

After a short stretch of industrial buildings you cross a stile into fine open country of water meadow and patches of woodland, following the former towpath for the next 4 miles along the river bank. At the third lock (East Lock), about $3\frac{1}{2}$ miles from Cannon Bridge, cross to the south bank of the river, recrossing at the large modern footbridge 700 m farther on.

The line of the path from the bridge lies clearly northward hugging the left-hand (western) side of the ditch and hedgerow. Go straight ahead with the orchard on your left, and through two gates eventually reaching a stile. Go over the stile and left past the farm buildings. After a few metres a waymark on a post directs you right between farm buildings to a stile and the roadway. Turn right, with the large mediaeval house, Barnes Place*, on your right, the path proceeding northwards again through the farm gate opposite (footpath sign).

Cross the footbridge which you come to on your left and then diagonally over the field to another footbridge. This leads to yet another bridge. Turn right over this bridge and follow the path along the bank of the stream, the river Bourne, that brings you to a roadway. Turn left passing a large house converted into two flats (Pierce Mill) and follow the narrow lane ahead.

Turn right at the T-junction where the road passes between a farm (Kent House Farm) and Kent House Place with its six oast houses converted into a residential complex. A short distance farther on the road bends to the right; at this corner, on your left, will be seen a concrete footpath sign. The path runs northwards from here for nearly a mile: a waymarked post shows the way to a white post and footbridge half-way along the path and through a vast orchard – a marvellous sight in apple-blossom time.

The road is reached by the side of a large corrugated iron barn of Crowhurst Farm. Bear left and then right in a few metres down a metalled access road to Peckham Place Farm (footpath sign and waymark). Keep left through the farm buildings and then take the path on the right that passes in front of two disused iron sheds. Continue through the two gates ahead and over the two bridges. The path runs along a wire fence in front of you. After 300 m you reach a stile in this fence; proceed left over the stile. Make for the left-hand tree of the line of trees on the field boundary ahead (a derelict cottage is about 50 m to your right). On reaching the tree there is a stile with a waymark directing you to the far left-hand corner of the next field (there is a tall conifer to guide you). Go through the gate on to the road (A26); cross over and to the right will be seen a stile with a footpath sign and waymark indicating the line of the path, following the field boundary and ditch to your left. This will bring you to a stile; from the stile a large tree should be visible in front of you with a white-painted blob on the trunk. A stile by this tree and a waymark show the direction across the next field to a narrow path between fences. At the end of this short stretch you arrive at the pleasant village of West Peckham*; turn left and it is only a few steps to the village green, ancient church, and the Swan pub and Post Office.

To continue, cross the village green to the kissing-gate in the far right-hand corner. The path is the track beside the high hedge bordering an orchard. You turn right at the bungalow, following the path where it later bears left along the field boundary, emerging on the road. Turn left on the road to a lodge on the opposite side. By the side of the lodge a footpath sign shows the Wealdway continuing over a bridge and along a wide track between two double lines of fine beech trees. Where the beeches end the path turns off on the right through a waymarked gate and along the left-hand (south) end of the field. A waymarked post then shows the route turning right to join a bridle-way rising gently for 600 m ending by the side of a white cottage. There is a fine view behind you from this bridle-way of the broad, fertile Medway valley you have just crossed.

Above the white cottage stands Gover Hill, owned by the National Trust. The path climbs the flank of the hill to the left from the NT sign across the road and runs parallel to and above the road forking right to Borough Green. The path then crosses a branch road running east-west with a footpath sign showing the direction you have to take (north-west) for the next 2½ miles through the western edge of Mereworth Woods*, an extensive Wealden forest area, here mainly coppice with an occasional lofty tree standing out as a landmark.

Carry straight on, ignoring the tracks crossing the route. After climbing gradually for about ¾ mile the path begins a long descent, eventually reaching a narrow roadway. Turn left on the road and go straight over the crossroads. Where the road ahead forks at Kettle Cottage take the right fork, Potash Lane. The lane runs along the eastern boundary of the attractive village of Platt*.

If you need refreshment and it is in opening hours, take the left fork at Kettle Cottage instead of the right. This will bring you to the centre of Platt with its church, the Blue Anchor inn and Post Office Stores. To rejoin the Wealdway, turn right out of the Blue Anchor or the Post Office and then left beyond the church; after 400 m you come to the far end of Potash Lane (see above).

At the far end of Potash Lane turn right and, in a few steps, left by a footpath sign down a narrow path between high hedges bordering the garden of the white house, Rough Acres. The path rises through Platt Woods. Follow the hurdle fence until at the top of the rise the route continues as a narrow path between fences (waymark) through conifers and clumps of rhododendrons. This soon emerges on to a road; turn left and descend the slope, passing Valley Cottage on your right. Just past the cottage there is a bridleway sign on the right. Follow this path through the trees and under a railway bridge to the main A20 road at Wrotham Heath.

Public transport

Wrotham Heath

Bus services Borough Green BR: Weekdays, frequent services; Sundays, approx. two-hourly. Gravesend–Meopham BR–Borough Green–*Wrotham Heath*–W. Malling BR–Maidstone: MD 10, 308. Weekdays, hourly; Sundays, two-hourly.

Platt

Bus services Buses serving Wrotham Heath (above) also serve Platt Flour Mill, $\frac{1}{2}$ mile from the Wealdway.

West Peckham

Bus services There are no public transport services serving West Peckham. Nearest bus stop is Mereworth, $1\frac{1}{4}$ miles. Services MD 900 Gillingham–Chatham–Maidstone–W. Malling BR–*Mereworth*–Tonbridge–Tunbridge Wells. Daily, two-hourly. MD 7. Maidstone–*Mereworth*–Tonbridge. Weekdays, hourly; Sunday: Maidstone–*Mereworth* and vice-versa only, two-hourly.

Barnes Street

Bus services Tonbridge: MD 207, 209. Weekdays only, hourly.

Tonbridge (see also Section 3)

British Rail Frequent services on weekdays, less frequent on Sundays. Services to London, Bromley, Orpington, Sevenoaks, Tunbridge Wells, Hastings, Dover, Ramsgate, Maidstone, Redhill, Guildford, Reading.

Bus services Barnes Street: MD 207, 209. Weekdays only, hourly. Borough Green (for Gravesend, Wrotham Heath, Platt): MD 222/3/4. Weekdays only, irregular (Mondays–Fridays: eight services daily; Saturdays: six services). Mereworth (for West Peckham): see above under West Peckham. Southborough Common (for Modest Corner): frequent, six minutes journey. Tunbridge Wells: frequent, fifteen minutes' journey.

Note MD = Maidstone & District. Service enquiries: telephone Borough Green (0732) 882128.

Accommodation

Tonbridge

Mrs L. M. Kirk	B&B.	¾ mile south-east of Cannon Bridge. Listed building.
Postern Forge	Evening meal if required.	
Postern Lane		
Tonbridge Kent		
TN11 0QU		
Telephone Tonbridge (0732) 352206		

Southborough

Mrs A. Moore	B&B.	Opposite Southborough Common. Convenient Modest Corner, Bidborough.
34 Pennington Road	Evening meal	
Southborough TN4 0SL	7 p.m.	
Telephone Tunbridge Wells (0892) 37986		

Tunbridge Wells
Tourist Information Centre: Town Hall. Telephone Tunbridge Wells (0892) 26121

Section 3

Tonbridge to **Fordcombe** 9½ miles

General description

From Tonbridge the first 2 miles of this section are for most of the
distance along the banks of the Medway, perhaps not such a
peaceful, rural stretch as the one you have just traversed on the
other side of Tonbridge but with its attractions nevertheless. You
will find this path asphalted for quite some way and in good weather
you will meet more people. This is only natural as this part of the
Wealdway is easily accessible to the quite densely populated
northern areas of Tonbridge and its neighbour, Hildenborough. The
route of the path passes through meadowland and woods and, with
the river only a few metres away, there is plenty to attract interest
and add to enjoyment: birds, bird-song, wild flowers and so on. In
May I particularly admired the different kinds of dragonflies.

The far end of the riverside footpath follows the bank of a new
'cut' that has been made as part of extensive flood-relief works. Just
where our path turns off, on the other side the Sevenoaks bypass,
the river has been dammed and a large basin formed: Hayesden
Water, used for sailing and recreation.

The Wealdway itself passes under the bypass (A21), the only
manmade feature of the section that intrudes on this otherwise
peaceful stretch of countryside. Once across the Medway you start
to climb out of the valley to the High Weald, reaching a height of
142 m (470 ft) at Bidborough where the splendid setting of the
church and the older houses clustered beneath reminded me of an
Alpine village particularly as – when I was there – there was the
scent of wood smoke in the air. The path now keeps to relatively
high ground for the greater part of its length except where the
Medway and smaller streams and their valleys are encountered.

You are now approaching the area of the Wealden iron industry.
Here were the iron-ore bearing sands and clays, trees for the
charcoal needed for the furnaces, and water to drive the hammers

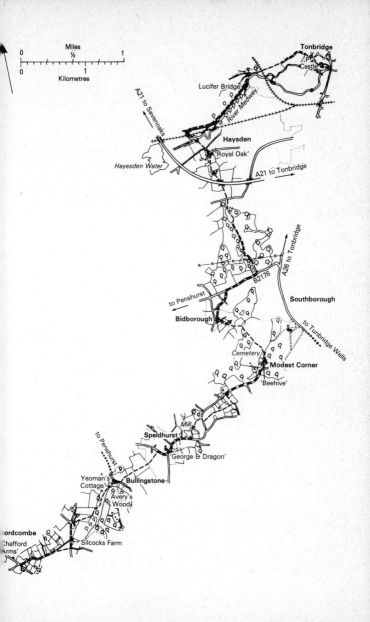

Tonbridge

Castle

Lucifer Bridge

River Medway

A21 to Sevenoaks

Haysden

'Royal Oak'

A21 to Tonbridge

Hayesden Water

B2176

A26 to Tonbridge

to Penshurst

Southborough

Bidborough

to Tunbridge Wells

Cemetery

Modest Corner

'Beehive'

Mill

Speldhurst

'George & Dragon'

to Penshurst

Yeoman's
Cottage

Bullingstone

Avery's
Wood

...ordcombe

'Chafford
Arms'

Silcocks Farm

Miles

0   ½   1

0   1

Kilometres

The gatehouse, Tonbridge Castle

and blast machinery, as explained in the chapter on background. There are several sites, invariably by small streams, to be found on the High Weald. Barden Furnace Farm, only 700 m north of the path at Speldhurst, is one of these and, later on, you will pass others even closer, with at least one dating from Roman times. Sandstone quarries by the side of the path may often be sources of the ore.

The path leads on through meadow and woodland, up hill and down dale, giving one or two sharp climbs. You come across some delightful buildings, for example the two splendid fifteenth-century cottages astride the path in Bullingstone Lane, and if you care to make a short diversion down the lane (see sketch map) there are two more historic homes: Tudor Cottage and Poundsbridge Manor – a photographer's dream. Although the villages are old they are not of such as ancient origin as others you have passed through to the north. This is because the High Weald was comparatively late in development. There is no mention of Bidborough or Fordcombe in the Domesday Book. The area was all forest which was gradually cleared for pig pasture and, from the late thirteenth century, iron-workings, unexploited since Roman days.

Speldhurst is not in Domesday but there is a mention in a Saxon document of the year 768. It was probably one of the many small seasonal settlements used in the autumn for pigs or wood-gathering for the benefit of a rich manor or abbey some miles farther north.

Two diversions are suggested: one to Tunbridge Wells and one to Penshurst. Tunbridge Wells, a considerable town of 50,000 people, owes its existence to a mineral spring, judged to be health-giving, discovered in the early seventeenth-century, so is a latecomer on the Kentish scene. A busy shopping centre, it still retains in the Pantiles and the streets nearby much of its eighteenth- and nineteenth-century charm – a good place for any shopping, refreshment or accommodation you may want.

Penshurst, the destination of the other suggested diversion, with its mediaeval courtyard outside the church, the Norman church itself and Penshurst Place, is one of the most attractive villages in the south of England. Penshurst Place has its unique and perfectly preserved fourteenth-century Great Hall and associations with that beloved Elizabethan poet and 'paragon of courtly and gentlemanly virtues', Sir Philip Sidney, whose birthplace and home it was.

MAPS
OS 1:50 000 188
OS 1:25 000 TQ 44/54

Route Southbound

The Wealdway continues from the north side of the Big Bridge over
the Medway in Tonbridge High Street, along Riverside Walk below
the towering south walls of Tonbridge Castle. Over to your left is a
recreation area with café, model railway and swimming-pool, but
keep straight on, joining the asphalted footpath signed 'Haysden
and Straight Mile' which follows one of the many rivulets draining
into the Medway for 800 m with a broad meadow on your left. The
main stream of the Medway is then joined after you have passed
under a railway bridge. Walk through some trees and then, turning
left over footbridges crossing two small streams, you continue on
the path, known from here as the 'Straight Mile'.

This is followed by a lovely stretch of the river on your left
through some woods full of bird-song in the spring. Do not cross the
large footbridge on the left shown on the map as Lucifer Bridge but
keep straight on along the river bank, eventually emerging into
meadowland and the new channel. Turn left over the footbridge
near the end of the 'cut', cross the small patch of field on the right
to the two waymarked culverts, go through the kissing-gate and
under the railway. Go through another gate (waymarked) and over
a footbridge, bearing left at the junction with another path. Cross
over two footbridges, joining a wide farm track to your right. This
leads to the road and straight ahead to the few houses forming the
hamlet of Haysden with its pub, the Royal Oak. You can get meals
and bar snacks here from Mondays to Saturdays (bar snacks on
Sundays).

At the Royal Oak bear right passing in front of the main entrance
to the pub – there is a concrete footpath sign at the side of this
access road. Continue down the access road past the cottages and
turn left at the bottom – there should be a waymark – and proceed
through the farmyard, bearing right. Go through the gate and cross
the field diagonally to the far left-hand corner where the entrance to
a tunnel under the Sevenoaks bypass will be seen. Go through the
tunnel, over the footbridge to the left and immediately right,
keeping the field hedge on your right, to a stile on the road ahead.

A stile with a footpath sign will be seen on the roadside opposite.
Over this stile, the Wealdway starts climbing the slope ahead

The Wealdway passing under the railway on the old course of the Medway

owards the crest of the Weald. On reaching a copse the path veers lightly to the right and through a waymarked gateway, continuing or some distance alongside a wood shown on the map with the urious name of Beechy Toll (according to the Oxford Dictionary toll' is a rare dialect word, used only in the south of England, for a vood). The path is 'sunken' as it nears the end, often indicating it is

New cut on the Medway near Haysden

of an ancient origin. The rather long climb ends in a stile on the B2176 Bidborough–Penshurst road and the village of Bidborough.

Turn right over the stile for a short walk along the road – most rewarding as you can enjoy as you walk (there is a pavement) a marvellous view of the Medway valley and the Weald beyond. On the other side of the road the gardens of the houses are resplendent

Farms on the Wealdway, Haysden

with rhododendrons and azaleas in May and early June. After about
500 m cross over to the south side of the road and next to the house
numbered 67 you will see the entrance to a footpath with a
waymark and sign to the church. The path makes its way zigzagging
through a modern estate. The eventual approach through the
churchyard to the church on its superb site overlooking the
surrounding country is an enchanting surprise.

View to the north from Bidborough

The earliest mention of Bidborough (Old English 'Bitta's mound or tumulus') is in 1114 but it is more than likely that there was a settlement here in pre-Conquest days. A church was here before 1218 as in that year the villagers asked for a priest to take regular services because the floods and swamps of the Medway below so often prevented them from walking to the church at Leigh, $2\frac{1}{2}$ miles

Steps hewn from the rock and lych gate Bidborough church

to the north. They got their wish and proceeded to improve their church; parts of their work are still visible in the roof beams and north aisle, as described in the interesting booklet available in the church. The local lords of the manor experienced the political vicissitudes of their times: Sir Thomas More – later executed by Henry VIII – lived in Great Bounds, pulled down 30 years ago to make room for the new estate. Sir Thomas invited his friend, Erasmus, to stay with him for a short while and the great Dutch scholar is said to have preached in the church. The Hare and Hounds pub on the main B2176 road past the footpath serves bar snacks from Mondays to Saturdays. You may make a diversion from here to Tunbridge Wells or Penshurst by bus (see pages 113–119).

The Wealdway proceeds, well waymarked, down the hill, Spring Lane, to the left past the village school, keeping straight on down the slope along the farm access road. Where the track turns left, carry straight on over a stile to the bottom of the slope and climb the quite steep gradient opposite. Go through a meadow and then along by the iron fence of the cemetery to the bottom of the next valley. A short climb brings you to some woodland; where the path forks, take the right-hand fork, coming out by a large house. Pass between the cottage with a white fence and the house on the right and you emerge on to the delightful open space among the woods, Modest Corner.

The Corner's modesty seems to keep it pretty private as even on a fine summer's day few people can be found there enjoying the pleasant seclusion. The old Beehive pub fits perfectly into the surroundings and you can get snacks there on Mondays to Fridays, to enjoy in its small garden or sitting on the common. You can make your diversion to Tunbridge Wells from here (see page 000).

To continue, pass down the slope in front of the Beehive, turning right on the country road below. Incidentally, the tiny stream at the bottom of the slope is the same kind of chalybeate (or iron-bearing) spring as that to which Tunbridge Wells owes its origin. Keep to the country road up the hill and after about 800 m you come to a metal gate with a footpath sign on the left opposite the drive to the Birketts. With hedge on your right and then fields the path continues as far as the boundary of the second field, with a kissing-gate on the left. Do not go through the gate but turn sharp right along the boundary hedge (there is a waymark on the large telephone post by the gate). Follow along the field edge until you

Modest Corner: Beehive pub in background

arrive at a stile and steps leading down to the road.

Turn right on the road and, in a few steps, on the left will be seen a stile with a footpath sign. Take this path, over a second stile and down a short steep slope to a stream and former mill with mill pond. Continue up the access track which brings you out on the road leading up the hill on the right to the church and the centre of the village of Speldhurst.

Speldhurst village

As mentioned, Speldhurst is not in Domesday probably because there was no permanent settlement being tilled that could be worth anything. The entry in the Anglo-Saxon document of 768 refers no doubt to a seasonal swine pasture or clearing for timber felling (Speldhurst – Old English 'hill where wood chips are taken'). It is another hill-top village; the church, in a fine position, is a Victorian building replacing a Norman one destroyed by lightning. The stained glass by the Pre-Raphaelites, Burne Jones and William Morris, is much admired. The fine old George and Dragon inn opposite the church actually has some fourteenth-century beams. You can get meals and bar snacks here daily, including Sundays. The Post Office Stores is a few metres down the road past where the Wealdway turns off south.

Follow the main road that circles the church. About 200 m on the left-hand side is an iron gate and footpath sign indicating the path to take. At first heading between the backs of houses and gardens and then over an open meadow with fine views towards the north, the path finishes through some trees down to a country lane (Bullingstone Lane). Bear right down the lane and in a few steps the path continues on the left between two splendid small fifteenth-century thatched yeomen's cottages, both bearing the plaque of the Kent County attesting their historic origin. The owner of one of them informed me that his cottage, built in about 1460, still bears traces where the smoke escaped through the roof before the days of chimneys.

If you are interested in old dwellings such as these and have not time to make the diversion to Penshurst, there are two gems within 800 m: keep on Bullingstone Lane and you will come firstly to Tudor Cottage (also with the plaque) and then at the crossroads the rather bizarre Poundsbridge Manor (1593). See page 000.

From Bullingstone Lane you can make the diversion on foot over the fields to Penshurst. See page 000.

The path between the two cottages leads down through a wood, Avery's Wood, over a small stream (keep to the right-hand track) and on for about 500 m to a stile (waymarked). Go over the stile and across the meadow, making for the far left-hand corner where there are two more waymarked stiles before you come to the road by two ponds.

Turn left on the road (Cooper's Lane) and go straight ahead. Keep in the same direction, passing the farm Silcock's on the left

Footbridge in Avery's Wood near Fordcombe

and Glebe House on the right. Opposite the road turning on the left
will be seen an iron gate with the Wealdway waymark and some
steps. The path crosses a field – a hard tennis court is on the left –
and finishes at a stile on the roadway. Turn left on the road and,
passing some cottages with good views to the north, you arrive at
the crossroads in Fordcombe.

Fordcombe village

Fordcombe (Old English 'valley of the fir trees') is first mentioned in a document of 1313 and is therefore of recent origin compared with most of the other villages on the Wealdway! The centre of the present village was built by the local landowner, Lord Hardinge, a former Governor General of India, in the middle of the last century. The inn, the Chafford Arms, is named after earlier lords of the manor and the sign shows a trader crossing the ford over the Medway nearby on an old pack-horse route through Kent. The inn serves meals and bar snacks daily except Christmas Day! Post Office Stores open daily except Sundays.

Route Northbound

From the crossroads in the centre of Fordcombe* take the road going eastwards signed 'Poundsbridge and Speldhurst'. After passing cottages – there is a fine view to the left – go over the stile (waymarked) on the right and across the field with a hard tennis court to the right of the path. Go down some steps and on to the road and turn left, passing the farm Silcock's on the right. You come to a fork in the road: on the right, opposite the sign 'Cooper's Lane', there is a waymarked stile: this is the next stretch to follow. The path takes you between two ponds and then over two stiles. Note the warning that dogs must be kept on a lead. Cross the field diagonally to the far left-hand corner to another waymarked stile at the edge of the wood.

The route then follows a clear path to the left through the very pleasant Avery's Wood. After dipping to cross a small stream the path emerges on to the country lane, Bullingstone Lane.

Note the two most attractive thatched cottages on either side of the path. These are fifteenth-century yeomen's dwellings and both bear the Kent County Historic Building plaque. From this point you can make a diversion to Penshurst* (see page 116). See also the note on page 107 regarding two more historic houses nearby in Bullingstone Lane.

From the path between the two cottages turn right and in a few steps, on the left, is a footpath sign and waymark indicating the path which crosses two fields – with fine views over the Weald to the north – and then leads between fences on to the road in the village of Speldhurst*.
You can make a diversion to Tunbridge Wells* by bus from here (see page 114).

Turn right, following the road round the church and down the hill on the right (the Tunbridge Wells road). At the bottom of the hill turn left past the large white house, Brook House, and along the access road to the former mill. Go through the yard, across the mill stream and up the steep slope on the other side and you will reach, at the top, two stiles bringing you to the road.

Turn right on this road and in a few metres farther on, on the left, are some steps and a stile. These lead to a path through fields for about 500 m. When you come to an iron kissing-gate do not go through the gate but turn sharp left along the hedgerow (there is a waymark on the telephone post by the gate). The path will bring you to an iron gate on to a road. You turn right down the hill; at the bottom, just past the road on the left to the cemetery, there is a path on the left leading up past a cottage. This will bring you to the very pleasant Modest Corner* and the little Beehive pub on the green.

You can make a diversion to Tunbridge Wells* from here (see page 114).

The path proceeds past the pub and turns to the left down the track between a house and the cottage with the white-painted fence. The track is the start of a bridle-way through the wood. Where the path forks, turn down the left fork to a stile. The route continues to the cemetery seen ahead and runs along by its iron fence. At the top of the slope you cross a meadow and down through some trees to another rise opposite, emerging on to an access road that brings you to the church and the centre of the village of Bidborough*.

Climb up to the church and follow the asphalt path through the churchyard to a gate. The path runs from this gate, past the cricket ground on the right and then through a modern estate, eventually bringing you out on the B2176 Bidborough–Penshurst Road. Turn right on this road, from which you can enjoy some splendid views, and after about 400 m the Wealdway continues on the left over a stile (footpath sign and waymark) and down the long wooded slope, still giving you a fine view. At the bottom of the slope there is a stile to cross and, on the other side of the road, another one. The path runs along the field edge in front of you until a footbridge is seen on your left. Go over this bridge and on the right through the tunnel under the Sevenoaks bypass (A21). Once through the tunnel bear left and cross the field diagonally to the left-hand corner; go through the gate and farm buildings, emerging on the access road; turn right and you come to the Royal Oak* pub at Haysden.

Bear left along the road but where it bends to the left keep straight on along the farm track; after 200 m there is a path taking you over a series of footbridges and under the railway. On the other side of the railway, go through the gate and, bearing right, make for the large footbridge over the new 'cut' on the Medway. Turn right when you get over this bridge and join the path that continues for the most part along the Medway without deviating to the left or right all the way for 2 miles to Tonbridge.

Diversions

(a) *Tunbridge Wells*. Mileage 8 miles by bus (urban walking).
A busy town of 50,000 inhabitants, Tunbridge Wells owes its origin to a supposedly health-giving chalybeate spring discovered in the early seventeenth century by a local nobleman who became enthusiastic about the good it had done him. Its popularity really began when Charles I and Queen Henrietta Maria came down here so that she could convalesce after the birth of her first son. Many years later Charles II, the son, followed his mother's lead and from then on the 'nobility and gentry' from London and the shires flocked to take the waters and generally disport themselves, delighted by the beauty of the surroundings and the facilities that sprang up, including gaming houses and theatres. The coming of the turnpike road in 1710 linking the town with the first good road from London increased its popularity. The fact that in 1735 Beau Nash was invited to become the spa's Master of Ceremonies and organise everything, and that he graciously accepted, is a token of Tunbridge Wells' reputation as a centre of recreation and fashion.

The coming of the railway in 1845 continued its rapid growth not only as a resort but also as a pleasant place of residence. Many of the shops and houses built in the early 1800s still survive and form the main attraction: the charming Pantiles (to the south of the town by the main A26 road), a terrace of shops and buildings near the famous spring, was first built by Queen Anne in 1699 but was rebuilt 100 years later. A pleasant half-hour can be spent walking round the area. The water of the spring no longer claims to have any particularly good properties but you can still drink a glass for a small fee; the spring is near the Pantiles.

The extensive common in the heart of the town is preserved in perpetuity for the use and enjoyment of the public and is a most pleasant place to linger in. There are many inns and eating places and you can always find accommodation. The Tourist Information Centre (telephone Tunbridge Wells (0892) 26121) is at the Town Hall and will help with any information required. The Bus Information Office is nearby in Mount Pleasant Road, as is the Town Museum.

Directions for southbound walkers
As Tunbridge Wells comprises a built-up area of nearly 4 miles from north to south, and as only a small part in the south of the town is of historical interest, the use of the bus services is suggested as an alternative to the purgatory of walking along a main road. The alternatives using bus services are:

From Bidborough Instead of turning right when you get to the B2176 in Bidborough turn left and in 400 m you come to the main A26 road and the Maidstone & District bus stop, Bidborough Corner. The service is frequent on weekdays, not so frequent on Sundays (about half-hourly).

From Modest Corner Instead of turning right down past the Beehive pub, keep straight on along the north of the green; in about 800 m you reach the busy A26 at Southborough Common. There is a frequent bus service (served by the same buses as Bidborough Corner above).

To rejoin the Wealdway, take the bus back to Southborough Common and walk to Modest Corner. Alternatively, there is an infrequent service from Tunbridge Wells central bus station to Speldhurst (weekdays only) or Fordcombe.

Cricket on Southborough Common

Directions for northbound walkers
There are infrequent bus services (weekdays only) to Tunbridge
Wells from Fordcombe and Speldhurst, or you can walk the 800 m
from Modest Corner to Southborough Common (see above) and
take the frequent bus from there to Tunbridge Wells.

To rejoin the Wealdway, take the bus from Tunbridge Wells to

Bidborough Corner then walk the short distance along the B2176 towards Bidborough village. The waymarked stile is on the right leading down the slope.

(b) *Penshurst*. Extra walking mileage 4 miles out and back the same route.

Penshurst is one of the jewels in the Kentish crown. The stately home Penshurst Place is renowned not only as a handsome ancient English family seat whose original fourteenth-century Great Hall is in essentially the same condition as when it was built and as when Queen Elizabeth I was entertained there, but also for its associations. Penshurst is inseparable from thoughts of that poet and beau-ideal of Elizabethan times, Sir Philip Sidney, who was born and lived there and must have written many of his incomparable verses in the house. Elizabeth and her court were shattered by his death at the age of 32 in the siege of Zutphen and wore mourning for three months. The States General of the Netherlands asked that he should be buried in their country and promised a golden memorial. 100 years later the beauty of another Sidney, Dorothy, inspired the Cavalier poet Waller's verses to his sweet 'Sacharissa'.

The oak tree said by the poet Ben Jonson to have been planted at Philip Sidney's birth is shown in the grounds of Penshurst, where there is also a 'Sacharissa's Walk'. The venerable church of St John the Baptist is Norman and contains monuments going back to the thirteenth century.

As explained in the excellent booklet on sale in the church, Penshurst village and the country roundabout are full of interest. A still-surviving boundary survey made in 1289 lists a number of farms and manors nearby that flourish to this day, occupying the same sites as they did 700 years ago. It is a fascinating exercise to locate them on a present-day map, and generated in me a sense of the continuity and timelessness of our heritage.

The Leicester Arms (the Earls of Leicester were the forebears of the family still living in Penshurst) and the Spotted Dog are the two hostelries where meals and snacks are available, and there are also two teashops in the village. Penshurst Place is open to the public daily except Mondays (open Spring and Summer Bank Holidays) from April to the first Sunday in October: the grounds from 12.30 to 6 p.m. and the house from 1 to 5.30 p.m. The Post Office is by the church.

Directions for south- and northbound walkers
For the 2-mile walk mainly across fields to Penshurst, at Bullingstone Lane (between Speldhurst and Fordcombe: see page 95) turn north along the lane (by the two historic thatched cottages). After 800 m you pass Tudor Cottage, another cottage with a Kent County Historic Building plaque. At the crossroads there is the well-preserved timbered Poundsbridge Manor bearing the date 1593 and 'WD' in large letters. The initials – very much larger than is usually the case, perhaps giving clue to the reverend gentleman's character – are those of William Dartnoll, rector of Penshurst for over 30 years from 1563–96. 'Eta 69' gives his age – another unusual feature. He had only three more years to enjoy his brand-new residence as he died in 1596. You can find out all about him on a tablet in Penshurst church. The family is mentioned in 1491 and descendents, Durtnells the Builders of Brasted, founded in 1591, claim to be the oldest firm in England.

Opposite the manor (also known as the Picture House) is a concrete footpath sign and stile. Cross this stile and turning immediately left follow the field boundary. Turn half-right on entering the next field and cut diagonally to the left-hand bottom corner, where a five-barred gate and a pedestrian gate will be seen. Go through this gate, taking the path alongside the ditch on your right. The path leads to a gated footbridge over the Medway, quite a small stream here. Continue straight on, with a wire fence on your left. At the end of the fence go through the gap in the hedge ahead and slightly to the right of you. Turn right and follow the field edge and then where it turns left along the river. At the right-hand bend in the river turn right, over a plank crossing the ditch (close to a World War II pillbox); follow the field boundary and the river for 500 m and then cross the footbridge.

Turn left over the bridge and follow the path round the extensive hop-garden. After about 200 m the track leaves the riverside and

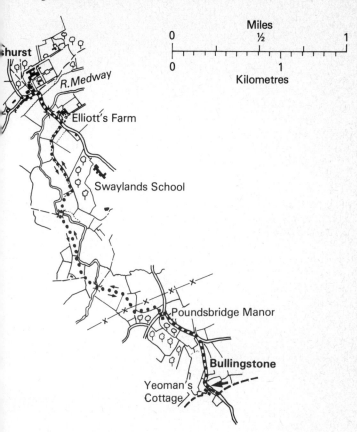

turns right up the slope, bending eventually to the left along a clear
farm track, which brings you out on the road. There is a good view
of Penshurst church and village from the track. Turn left on the road
and, passing some almshouses (1633), in a few minutes you will be
in the centre of Penshurst where 'Leicester Square', the church and
the Leicester Arms make a fine mediaeval composition.

    You can rejoin the Wealdway by the same route as outward, or
there are possible buses – see below.

Penshurst village

There are other ways of taking in Penshurst. For southbound walkers there is a two-hourly bus service (weekdays only) from Bidborough or Tunbridge Wells; rejoin on foot as above or by the two-hourly bus service (weekdays only) to Fordcombe. For northbound walkers there is a two-hourly weekday bus service from Fordcombe to Penshurst; rejoin the Wealdway on foot as above or by the two-hourly weekday bus to Bidborough.

Public transport

Tonbridge (see also Section 2)

British Rail See Section 2.
Bus services Southborough (for Modest Corner): frequent, six
minutes' journey. Tunbridge Wells: frequent, fifteen minutes'
journey. Medway Towns–Maidstone–*Stone Cross*–E. Grinstead:
MD 900. Daily, two-hourly.

Tunbridge Wells

British Rail Frequent daily services, London (Charing Cross)–
Orpington–Sevenoaks–*Tunbridge Wells*–Hastings. Also serves
many more destinations via Tonbridge.
Bus services Bidborough: MD 233. Weekdays only, two-hourly.
(Bidborough village can also be reached from Bidborough
Corner, 1 mile, on the Tunbridge Wells–Southborough–
Tonbridge route.) Tonbridge: frequent, fifteen minutes' journey.
Fordcombe: MD 231. Weekdays only, two-hourly. Speldhurst:
MD 289. Weekdays only, approx. two-hourly. Medway Towns–
Maidstone–*Stone Cross*–E. Grinstead: MD 900. Daily, two-
hourly. Withyham: MD 291. Weekdays, two-hourly; Sundays,
two services only. Crowborough–*Poundgate (Ashdown Forest)*–
Uckfield–Brighton: SD 729. Weekdays, hourly; Sundays, two-
hourly.

Note MD = Maidstone & District. Service enquiries: telephone
Borough Green (0732) 882128.
SD = Southdown. Service enquiries: telephone Brighton (0723)
606600.

Accommodation

Southborough See Section 2

Fordcombe

Daneby Hall	B&B.	On route.
The Lane	Evening meal	Vegetarian
Fordcombe	7 p.m.	(meals also
Tunbridge Wells		available village
Kent TN3 0RP		inn)
Telephone Fordcombe		
(089274) 235		

Tunbridge Wells
Tourist Information Centre: Town Hall.
Telephone Tunbridge Wells (0892) 26121

Section 4

Fordcombe to **Ashdown Forest** (Camp Hill) 10 miles

General description
This section is fine open country – you pass through only one village, Withyham, on the whole of the 10 miles. Here again is great variety: just south of Stone Cross is, to my mind, one of the most beautiful parts of the Wealdway, and from the top of Ashdown Forest you have the finest views in the south-east. From Stone Cross you are walking, for over a mile, high up in a rolling countryside of green fields and wooded slopes with not a human habitation in sight. You are here seeing the last of the Kentish stretch of the Wealdway, and a fine farewell scene it makes (and a fine introduction for those coming from the south). The boundary in the Medway valley, where the path crosses from Kent into East Sussex, is the smallest of streams, the Grom, flowing into the Medway a short distance to the west. Presumably, when most of the boundaries were laid down by the Saxons 1000 years ago, the stream was a more impressive waterway or the area was a swampy barrier.

There is no difference immediately discernible in the terrain of the two counties but from Withyham, a couple of miles farther on, the path begins to climb almost imperceptibly to the highest point on the Wealdway, Greenwood Gate Clump on Ashdown Forest. You pass through Five Hundred Acre Wood, a most extensive tract of beech, oak and conifers, originally part of the Ashdown Forest heathland but enclosed 300 years ago and planted with trees. A wonderful place to walk through, it is full of bird-song in the spring.

From Five Hundred Acre Wood you emerge on to Ashdown Forest. This wild stretch of heath is full of interest. Measuring about 8 miles from east to west and the same distance at its widest from north to south, it is all that remains of the Forest of Anderida, known to the Romans. Said by the Saxons to be 120 miles long, the area was energetically cleared until, by the time the Normans arrived, the only region not settled was the highest ground with the poorest soil: the Forest of Ashdown.

The Romans and the Celts before them had extracted iron from the iron-bearing sands and the Romans built roads for its transport – we shall see fascinating traces of these. However it was not until well after the Norman Conquest, at the end of the thirteenth century, that settlement of the Forest began in the 15,000 acres or so remaining. It was still pretty inaccessible – Edward I had to have five guides *en route* to Chichester in 1276 – and was divided among the large landowners as a hunting ground. It was from this time that the tussles between the owners and the Commoners began. The Commoners were those ordinary folk who had settled on the Forest and depended on it for a livelihood: for pasture for their pigs, wood for fuel and so on. Their struggles over 700 years have produced a unique historical solution: a triumph in many ways for justice, even if it has been a bit of 'rough justice' at times.

After a number of legal battles over the years, a Board of Conservators was set up in 1885. The Board consists of representatives of the local authorities and the Commoners (nowadays the residents on the Forest) and the titular 'owner', at present Lord De La Warr, and has authority over all matters involving the protection of the Forest, Commoners' rights, etc. The rights, dating from time immemorial, still include 'estover' (gathering of wood for fuel) and 'pannage' (putting the pigs or sheep out to graze on the Forest on payment of one pig or sheep in ten), although pannage is seldom claimed nowadays.

The area – 6500 acres – over which the Commoners' rights were claimed were confirmed as common land and therefore the right of access by the public was also protected. We must be grateful for the Commoners' struggles over the centuries that have preserved for us this marvellous expanse of open country over which we can wander at will.

Within a mile or two of the Wealdway there are Forest sites of the Wealden iron industry that flourished from the fourteenth century for 200 years and must have accounted for the disappearance of most of the remaining trees at that time; one of these sites goes back to Roman times.

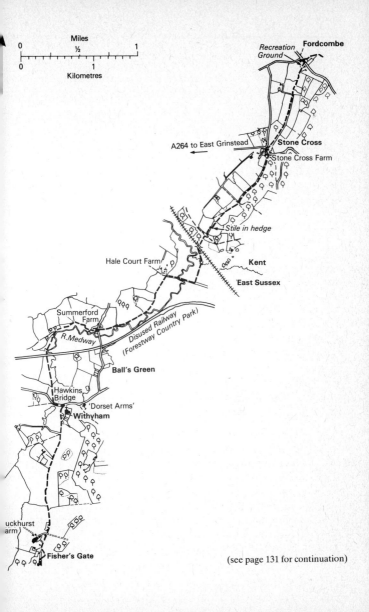

Miles

Kilometres

Recreation
Ground **Fordcombe**

A264 to East Grinstead **Stone Cross**

Stone Cross Farm

Stile in hedge

Hale Court Farm

Kent

East Sussex

Summerford
Farm

R.Medway

Disused Railway
(Forestway Country Park)

Ball's Green

Hawkins
Bridge

'Dorset Arms'
Withyham

uckhurst
arm

Fisher's Gate

(see page 131 for continuation)

The natural history of Ashdown Forest is in many ways unique, and Garth Christian's book *Ashdown Forest* gives fascinating details of the wild life, plants and wild flowers to be found there, including the birds and butterflies.

On a practical note, as Withyham is the only place *en route* on this section where refreshments or food are available you should make your plans accordingly.

MAPS
OS 1:50 000 188
OS 1:25 000 TQ 44/54, 42/52

Route Southbound

When you reach the crossroads in Fordcombe turn left. There is a recreation ground on the right, and through a gap in the hedge will be seen the path to take, signposted to Ashurst. Cross the recreation ground diagonally to the stile in the far left-hand corner. The route continues straight on, over stiles, keeping to the field boundaries, unfortunately likely to be rather overgrown in the summer. There are fine views to the right. After ¾ mile you come to the main A264 East Grinstead–Tunbridge Wells road at Stone Cross, a hamlet of a few houses and a farm – no pub or shop.

Turn left on the road and at the corner where it bends sharply left – beware of the traffic – the signposted and waymarked entrance to the next stretch of the Wealdway is visible on the right, beside the house, Stone Cross Lodge. At first between fences, the path emerges into some fine rolling country of wood and field. The route lies straight ahead, following the contour just below the crest of the ridge, the view widening to reveal a splendid picture of hill and valley.

The land eventually slopes down to the floor of the valley ahead. Another path branches off the Wealdway at the top of the slope but our path keeps to the left down the incline. About half-way down there is a stile in the hedgerow on the right; cross this into the next field turning left down the slope, keeping to the field edge. Go through the small copse to a track running east-west (this is the

View from near Stone Cross

Sussex Border Path). Turn right on the track and, in a few metres, sharp left, passing through a white gate and under the railway.

On the other side of the railway there is another white gate. Bear left to a footbridge over the stream. This is the little river Grom (cf. Groombridge), here forming the boundary between Kent and East Sussex – it joins the Medway a short distance to the west. From the

Summerford Farm on the Wealdway near Withyham

footbridge the path continues slightly west of south to a wide access track that leads, to the right, over two bridges, towards the large farm (Hale Court Farm). Before reaching the farm, turn sharp left at the junction of paths, over the stile, signposted and waymarked.

From here the path follows the general direction of the Medway meandering pleasantly on your left, alternately curving to approach the path and then curving away to leave it. In about ¾ mile you come to a country road, opposite a farm, Summerford Farm. Cross the road and, to the left, the path leads over a stile, skirting the farm along the left-hand boundary, passing in front of Dairy Cottage behind the farm and continuing as a farm track.

The track proceeds some metres above the river, a most pleasing stretch with good views – the church spire to be seen in the distance is Hartfield church. Just before entering the copse ahead of you, where the river comes closest to the track, you have to descend the steep bank (there is supposed to be a path but it is not at all clear). From the bottom of the bank you bear half-left across the field to a footbridge over the river leading to stiles marking the crossing of the disused Forest Row–Groombridge railway line, now made into a public right-of-way (Forest Way Country Park).

The line of the path on the other side of the former railway track is straight ahead from the stile. It is not particularly clear, but if you make for a point just to the left of the barn seen in front you will come to a gate which is on the line of the footpath. Continuing in the same direction across the field, brings you to a gate on the B2110 Groombridge–Hartfield road. Turn left over the bridge.

The village of Withyham (Old English 'settlement of the willows') is a short distance along the road. A charming place, it is one of the mediaeval settlements resulting from the clearance of the Wealden forest, and its association with the great events of Britain and the USA is astonishing. It is the home of the Sackville family, whose ancestors came to England with William the Conqueror. They became Earls of Dorset (hence the Dorset Arms), the 1st Earl being not only Chancellor to Queen Elizabeth but also a poet of distinction, as was the 6th Earl (who was also a bit of a rake, as Pepys confirms). The Sackvilles were later allied through marriage with another great Sussex family, the Wests. Thomas West (1577–1618), 12th Baron De La Warr (or Delaware), was the Governor of the Virginia Company and founder of the States of Virginia and Delaware, giving his name also to the River and Bay. The poetic tradition of the Sackville-Wests was carried on until recent times through Victoria Sackville-West, a well-known novelist

The Dorset Arms, Withyham

and poet who died in 1962. Her memorial is in the church.

The splendid church, prominent as soon as you reach the road, is the 'history book' of the Sackvilles and De La Warrs. The Sackville family vault, resting place for fifteen generations, lies under the chapel and the monuments, works of some of the best artists of the time, are most impressive. The church was founded in the thirteenth century. The Norman building, except for the tower and north aisle, was destroyed by lightning in 1663 so most of the present building is seventeenth-century, as is the dignified rectory next door. Buckhurst Park, present home of the De La Warrs, is 800 m by the footpath leading up by the right-hand side of the Dorset Arms. In the sixteenth and seventeenth centuries it was the site of iron-workings of which there is no longer any trace except the lake (the furnace pond).

Withyham church was the scene recently of an unusual example of Anglo–American archaeological co-operation. It was reported in the *National Geographic Magazine* that American archaeologists excavating an early English settlement site in New England, destroyed with all its inhabitants by Indians, were shown in the Sackville vault a coffin-lid of the same pattern as one found on the American site. They had not been able previously to match this pattern from other American or English records. This discovery helped them to confirm certain dates in the story of the settlement.

The sixteenth-century Dorset Arms, in an ideal position in the village, serves bar snacks and meals every day including Sundays. The helpful Post Office Stores opposite is open on weekdays except Thursday and Saturday afternoons.

For the continuation of the Wealdway, after having turned left on the road as you came through the field gate, take the metalled access road on the right signed 'to the church'. This road is a through right-of-way for pedestrians only and leads for almost $1\frac{1}{2}$ miles through magnificent park-like countryside to Fisher's Gate (the 'Gate' is one of the entrances to Ashdown Forest). This road from Withyham is, incidentally, rather exposed to the elements. You keep to the roadway until you eventually reach cottages and farm buildings on the right and a white-painted gate ahead with the notice 'Private road. No through road. No footpath.'; you will see on the left a sign directing you to the footpath from here, running between fences through a thicket to a driveway. Turn right and follow this as it bears left, passing in a few metres a white cottage with 'church'-type windows. You are now in Five Hundred Acre Wood, of beech, oak and conifer, a part of Ashdown Forest that was

The Wealdway through Five Hundred Acre Wood. Two of the special Wealdway waymark posts can be seen

'enclosed' legally in 1693 for re-afforestation.

After passing the cottage keep to this main track which should bear more marks of use than any other track or path you come across. This main track dips down to a hollow past a large pond, backed by a handsome modern house.

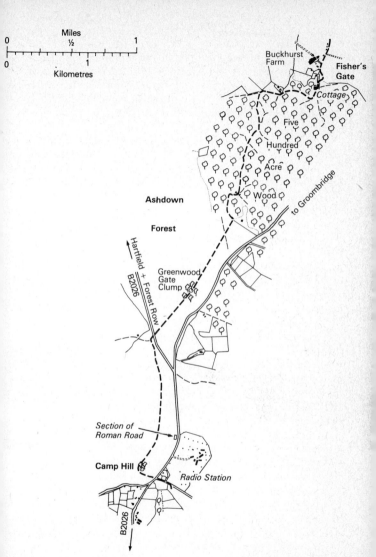

(see page 141 for continuation)

About 250 m farther on, where the track comes out to a field on the right, there are two five-bar gates. Opposite these gates turn sharp left down the wide forest track at right angles to the one you have been following. There is a footpath sign at the junction indicating this turning and some distance farther on a yellow waymark on a tree.

After 900 m down this forest track you arrive at a fence with a stile and a gate. As you cross the stile you will see on the far side one of the special waymarks that will guide you through the next 3 miles across Ashdown Forest. They are posts, 0.76 m (2ft 6in) high, with grooves cut in the top showing the line of the Wealdway in both directions – extremely useful. The route from the stile is clearly shown in this way and you will find similar posts, at reasonable distances apart, giving you confidence that you are on the right track.

The 'Forest' waymark posts bring you in about 600 m to the edge of the 'real' Ashdown Forest, the wild expense of rolling heathland. The exit path from Five Hundred Acre Wood turns sharply right. You can check on the position by looking left into the wood: there is a horse barrier and the exit is dead opposite.

Ashdown Forest, as you will see, is covered by tracks in all directions but the line of the Wealdway is made clear by the 'Forest' waymark posts at intervals. The track slopes upwards for about 800 m, with marvellous views in clear weather on both sides. You arrive at a clump of tall pines with a carved wooden sign, Greenwood Gate Clump. This is the highest point on the Wealdway (223 m–732 ft).

From Greenwood Gate Clump the Wealdway continues down the slope in a south-west direction, parallel to the B2188 on the left. You come to another road, the B2026, opposite a driveway signed to Old Lodge. Cross the road at this point to the entrance of the driveway, but turn half-left on an old track which, after 500 m, curves right, running parallel to the main B2026 road. Ahead of you to the right there is another prominent clump of conifer trees, Camp Hill, only a few metres lower than Greenwood Gate Clump, with a seat and a magnificent view. There is a café/teashop a short distance down the main road at Duddleswell.

Near Greenwood Gate Clump, Ashdown Forest

A section of the Roman Lewes–London road crossing Ashdown Forest is visible just off the Wealdway about 400 m before reaching Camp Hill. As you come abreast of the first (most northerly) mast of the large radio station on your left there is a wide track leading up on the left towards the main road, only 50 m away. Just before you get to the main road there is an enclosure, marked by a low wooden barrier, that contains the clear traces on the ground of the 'agger' running each side of the Roman roadway – there is an explanatory plaque at the site. The actual line of the Roman road continues northwards in the same direction to near where the Wealdway enters Five Hundred Acre Wood and then veers slightly left on its way through Edenbridge and across country to London Bridge.

Route Northbound

On the route of the Wealdway across Ashdown Forest a special type of waymark post (see page 132) indicates the line of the path at reasonable intervals.

From the summit of Camp Hill the route of the Wealdway will be seen curving away down a slight slope, running parallel to the main B2026 road with the tall masts of the radio station a few metres away on your right. (For the traces of the Roman road from Lewes to London see previous page). 1000 m from Camp Hill the B2026 turns north-west; our route turns half-left and crosses this main road by the entrance of a drive signed to Old Lodge. From there the line runs parallel to another main road, the B2188, towards a clump of tall pines surmounting a rise. This is Greenwood Gate Clump, the highest point on the Wealdway at 218 m (716 ft).

All along this stretch there are magnificent views over the wildest landscape in the south of England. From Greenwood Gate Clump the route continues northward, clearly indicated by the 'Forest' waymarks, parallel to the B2188 (the traffic can be heard but not seen – the vegetation is too dense at this point). Eventually Five Hundred Acre Wood is reached, a part of Ashdown Forest that was 'enclosed' in 1693 and is now a vast area of splendid beeches, oaks and conifers. The path – still marked with the special posts – turns left at first and then bears right, northwards through the wood. The 'Forest' waymarks cease at a stile but the last post shows clearly the direction from the stile for about 900 m northwards.

A T-junction of paths will be reached, nearly opposite two field gates. You turn right at this junction along the clear forest path, passing a clearing on the left with a large pond and attractive modern house in the background. Keep to the same path; ultimately

Camp Hill, Ashdown Forest, with section of the Roman Lewes–London road in foreground

you pass a white cottage on the left. You emerge on to a driveway; turn right and in a few metres, on the left, will be seen the sign to a footpath through a thicket that continues between fences across a field, bringing you out on a metalled private access road – it is a public right-of-way for walkers.

You are now clear of Ashdown Forest. Turn right along this road, past farm buildings and a few cottages and for the next 1¼ miles you have some fine walking through a park-like countryside of pasture and noble trees. The sight of Withyham church on a rise ahead of you indicates where your route reaches the Groombridge–Hartfield road. Turn left on the road, over the bridge and the continuation of the Wealdway is through the field gate on the right. There is a concrete footpath sign on the roadside.

If you have time to visit the village of Withyham*, turn right instead of left when you reach the motor road. In a few metres you have the old inn, the Dorset Arms, and the Post Office Stores. Withyham church is well worth a visit.

From the field gate mentioned above the line of the path runs across the field to a gate slightly to the right of the barn seen ahead. Go through this gate and, keeping the same direction, you come to a pair of stiles astride the disused Forest Row–Groombridge railway (now the Forest Way Country Park). Go over these stiles and make for the footbridge on the river, the Medway, in front of you. From the bridge bear half-right across the field towards the clump of trees and climb the steep bank in the trees on to a farm track (there is supposed to be a path up the bank but it is hard to find! It did not seem to be there, but it is not too hard a scramble). Turn right on the farm track running along the bank above the river – there are some very pleasant views over the countryside. You pass through the farmyard (Summerford Farm), in front of Dairy Cottage and out into the country road.
   Turn left on the road in front of the farm and go over the stile a few metres on the other side of the road to your right. The path then follows the valley with the Medway weaving its leisurely way to your right at a varying distance from the path. You pass through two gates on the path and eventually reach a stile on the approaches to a farm (Hale Court Farm). Turn right on the access road leaving the farm on your left. You cross two concrete bridges: immediately past the second one turn left across the field towards the railway embankment, over a footbridge (the small stream is the River Grom, here the Sussex–Kent boundary). Bear right and pass under the railway.

From the railway bridge, go straight forward towards the clump of trees. Turn right at the junction with the path crossing at right angles (this is the Sussex Border Path) and, in a few metres, go over the stile on the left and through the copse leading out into a field. Follow the field boundary on your right and you will come to another stile in the hedge. Cross this stile, turn left up the slope and, from the crest of the rise, carry on in the same north-easterly direction following the contour, enjoying for the next 1000 m splendid views of the Weald to your right. The path finishes between narrow fences to bring you to the main A264 Tunbridge Wells–East Grinstead road at Stone Cross (no shop or facilities).

Turn left on the main road. Round the bend and in a short distance on your right is the junction with the country road signposted to Fordcombe. At this junction there is a patch of open ground on the right. On the far side, to the left of two white cottages, there is a stile and waymark. Cross the stile. The route of the path now follows straight ahead across fields for $\frac{3}{4}$ mile finishing at the recreation ground in Fordcombe*. Cross the ground diagonally to the left to the gap in the hedge by a large oak tree. Turn left on the road to the crossroads.

Public transport

Fordcombe

Bus service Tunbridge Wells: MD 231. Weekdays only, two-hourly.

Stone Cross

Bus service Medway Towns–Maidstone–West Malling–
    Tonbridge–Tunbridge Wells–*Stone Cross*–East Grinstead–
    Gatwick: MD 900. Daily, two-hourly.

Withyham

Bus service Tunbridge Wells–*Withyham*–E. Grinstead: MD 291.
  Weekdays, two-hourly; Sundays, two services only.

Ashdown Forest (Camp Hill)

Bus services Uckfield SD 119, 149. Irregular and infrequent (from
  Poundgate, 1¼ miles east of Camp Hill) SD 729: Tunbridge
  Wells–Crowborough–*Poundgate*–Uckfield–Lewes–Brighton.
  Weekdays, hourly; Sundays, two-hourly.

Note MD = Maidstone & District. Service enquiries: telephone
  Borough Green (0732) 882128.
SD = Southdown. Service enquiries: telephone Brighton (0723)
  606600.

Accommodation

Fordcombe See Section 3.

Fairwarp (Ashdown Forest) See Section 5.

Section 5

Ashdown Forest (Camp Hill) to **Blackboys** 8½ miles

General description

From the summit of Camp Hill the Wealdway begins a gradual descent and most of this section is still in Ashdown Forest territory. Here you get a more 'intimate' aspect of the Forest. Instead of the breezy, bare uplands and wide tracks of Greenwood Gate Clump or Camp Hill you can find yourself on narrow sandy tracks, almost obscured by the bracken after a summer's growth, and you thank your stars for the 'Forest' waymarks always there at strategic spots to guide you. The route is almost entirely rural, avoiding all villages and urban centres, with the exception of the small collection of houses at Five Ash Down, until you reach Blackboys. You can however make short diversions – as mentioned in the text – to Fairwarp, Buxted or Uckfield if in need of refreshment or accommodation.

The terrain you pass through is full of variety and colour, changing from heath to woodland and from wood to heath again a number of times. In spring and summer the bright green of the bracken contrasts with the colours of the wild flowers; in autumn the golden glow of the dying ferns and the tints of the heather take their place. Occasionally you come across an attractive house or cottage, fitting perfectly into the scene.

The number of small narrow valleys, or 'gills', made by the streams flowing off the heights of Ashdown Forest were ideal spots for iron-workings and we come across some of these. There was ore-producing rock in abundance; the streams were dammed (the dams were called 'bays') to provide water power and the surrounding woods were sources for the charcoal for the furnaces. There is little to see nowadays but Furnace Wood is on the path and there is a kind of quarry that was probably a source of iron-stone. The discovery of a site at Oldlands Farm at the north end of Furnace Wood 150 years ago makes fascinating reading. In 1848 the observant Rector of Maresfield while out walking on the main road near Fairwarp (see page 143) noticed workmen using cinders to repair the road. Among the cinders were pieces of Roman pottery. The workmen told him the cinders came from a field at Oldlands Farm nearby. On investigation he found there was an area of 6 acres with a bed of cinders up to 3 m deep and that the remains of a Roman building had been unearthed with pottery, skeletons and coins. The coins showed that the period of the iron-workings was that of the Emperor Vespasian (69–79 AD), i.e. the earliest period of the Roman occupation of Britain.

From the beginning of the fifteenth century there were also extensive iron-works on the Oldlands estate. These were fed by a large pond and dam (marked as 'Pond Bay' on the 1:25 000 Ordnance Survey map). This is on private land and not on view but you can see the stream and the farm nearby close to the Wealdway (see page 143). Some, at least, of the iron produced was used for the first cannon to be made in England by the Rector of Buxted in 1543 and from this time the Weald had a virtual monopoly for 200 years. Hume the historian said that 'shipbuilding and the founding of iron were the sole arts at which England excelled. They seem indeed, to have possessed alone the secret of the latter.' One of the Wealden cannon, bearing the initials 'JF' of John Fuller, a Heathfield iron-founder, is in the Tower of London. It seems incredible that up to about 250 years ago – in the lovely setting of Oldlands, for example – furnaces were blazing and smoking, water-wheels turning and huge hammers clanging, all helping to make the best cannon in the world. Just another Wealdway dividend!

Leaving Ashdown Forest behind, you approach the flatter ground of the Low Weald crossing Buxted Park, another of the county's famous estates. From here you are close enough to Uckfield to make a diversion if desired. From Buxted Park the route continues with only one gradient of any length, following dawdling streams across fields until Blackboys is reached, offering an old pub for food and refreshment and a youth hostel for accommodation.

On the whole stretch from Camp Hill to Blackboys it pays to keep your eyes and ears open as you walk. Hearing and watching a redstart and dozens of dragonflies on a beautiful summer evening

Camp Hill
The Crow's
Nest

Brown's Brook Cottage

Romany Cottage
Oldlands Corner

Forester
Arms
Roman Foundry site

Furnace Wood

Fairwarp

Hendall Manor

Cottage

Hendall Wood

Five Ash Down
Garage

Five Ashes Inn
The Oast Farm

to Uckfield
School
Hogg House
R. Uck

Buxted Park
Buxted Place

to Uckfield

Mill
Hempstead Farm

Pond
*continued
above*

Shawford Farm
YH
Tickerage
Mill

Gatehouse
Green Farm
Cottage
B2102

Blackboys

Miles
0   ½   1

0   1
Kilometres

near Fairwarp was quite exhilarating.

As far as conditions are concerned, walking through bracken in damp weather can soon soak your boots and legs; those with bare legs should watch out on the narrow heath paths for brambles. The fields from Buxted Park onwards can be muddy in wet weather.

A short diversion from Buxted Park to Uckfield is described at the end of this section.

MAPS
OS 1:50 000 188, 198, 199
OS 1:25 000 TQ 42/52

Route Southbound

From Camp Hill the direction of the Wealdway turns sharp left, with the trig point (198 m–650 ft) on your right towards the B2026 main road. You should emerge at the junction with the minor road running east alongside the south wire fence of the radio establishment. There is a cottage at the junction. In about 150 m on this road, a 'Forest' waymark on the south side marks the continuation of the path following a clear track through gorse bushes and bracken with some good views over the fields to the right.

After 450 m on the path, cross over the stile and turn right on the farm track that bends to the left past a modern villa. Follow this track, through the gate, until, where the track makes a sharp bend to the right, you will see on the left in the hedge by an oak tree a stile with a waymark. Go over this stile, turning right to another stile. The line from here is shown by a 'Forest' waymark post, leaving the bungalow on your right. Keep a sharp lookout on the right for the next waymark post indicating the path that crosses the driveway *en route* and then dips down through the bracken.

You come to a small cottage in a hollow. The path circles the cottage to the left rather awkwardly, with a waymark showing the direction. Having negotiated the cottage look out carefully for the next waymark post, in the grass, on the other side of the rear driveway of the cottage, showing the path leading down through the wood.

On coming to the far boundary of the wood, cross the footbridge, turning left past the tall holly hedge of Brown's Brook Cottage. Pass in front of the house and the cottages on to the metalled access road with its 'sleeping policemen' (humps made in the surface to restrict car speeding). Between the first two humps, on the right, there is a 'Forest' waymark indicating where the path leads up the bank, over a private driveway and, as a narrow path through the bracken, to a very wide bridle-way track across the heath.

Turn left on this track: 160 m farther on will be seen a 'horse-head' bridle-way sign. Just beyond this, on the right, is the sign for the next stretch of the Wealdway, snaking its narrow way across the bracken-covered heath for the next 800 m. Waymark posts at strategic spots are a great help.

The path brings you out by a white house, Oldlands Corner, facing the handsome iron gates of Oldlands Hall, decorated with ornate coats-of-arms.

This corner, with its surrounding fields and trees, is one of the most attractive spots on the Wealdway. It is difficult to believe that from the sixteenth to the eighteenth century it was part of Britain's 'Black Country' as one of the busiest centres of the Sussex iron industry with furnaces aflame, water-wheels splashing and hammers clanging. Centuries earlier the Romans were smelting iron here and it was in a field nearby, alongside the Wealdway that the deposits of slag from their workings up to a depth of 3 m were found 150 years ago. The iron from here was used to make the first cannon in England in 1543 for Parson Levett of Buxted (see page 147).

Bear right along the country road. On your left, across the fields, is Furnace Wood, its name indicating the connection with age-old former local industry. Recent excavations have proved that the fields lying between the road and Furnace Wood were the actual site of the huge deposits of Roman slag and ash as well as Roman coins and pottery discovered by the Rector of Maresfield in 1848. About 400 m down the road, on the left, is the entrance and gate to a sports field (keep straight on for a few metres for the village of Fairwarp and the Forester's Arms for refreshments and Post

Office). On the roadside by this entrance is the waymark post to a footpath through the thicket. Emerging on to a drive you will see on the left a waymarked gate to a field. Cross this field to a stile and a footbridge beyond. Cross the bridge and you are in Furnace Wood, now owned by the Forestry Commission. Turn right along the forest track. When you reach a wide track or fire-break across your path, go straight ahead – there should be a waymark – up a steep slope through the trees. There seems to be the remains of a quarry, possibly a former source of iron-stone, on the left (the Ordnance Survey 1:25 000 map shows a Pond Bay or former dam on the stream to the right).

On emerging from Furnace Wood, keep straight over the field towards the farm buildings ahead. Pass the cottage and turn right through the gate on to the driveway. Turn left, passing in front of the attractive Hendall Manor, also associated with the Wealden iron industry, and then bear right on the metalled farm road for a few metres. A waymarked stile will be seen on the right at the bend in the road.

The path continues between hedges to a gate and stile with a waymark. Cross the field diagonally towards the right of the cottage seen in front of you where there is a gate. From the gate the line veers slightly to the left down the slope to the edge of a wood and another gate. The path climbs through this wood to a waymarked stile. Bear right across the field – a large tree is a guide – to a wire fence and through a small copse on to a minor road. Cross the road and a waymark shows the path through the gorse, parallel to the road on your left. Follow the signs and you come out on this main A26 Uckfield–Crowborough road.

This is the featureless hamlet of Five Ash Down. The Five Ashes Inn (meals and bar snacks served daily including Sundays) and the Post Office Stores (open every day except Thursday and Sunday afternoons) are 300 m down the road to the right.

Cross the road and the path continues along the right-hand wall of the garage to a kissing-gate and from there straight on, keeping to the field boundaries on your right and crossing a couple of stiles,

Hendall Manor on the Wealdway near Five Ash Down

until you pass a farm shop on your left, coming to the A272 Haywards Heath–Buxted Road.

Turn left on the main road, cross the bridge over a stream and go up the hill. Near the top of the rise, on the right, is a drive signed 'To the Church of St Margaret the Queen. AD 1250'. This is the entrance to Buxted Park, through which the Wealdway runs for the

Hogg House, Buxted Park, home of the iron-founder, Ralph Hogg. Note the Hogg crest below the centre window

next mile – and a magnificent park it is. Criss-crossed by public footpaths it is a fine place for exploring at leisure.

The park entrance is of appropriate dignity, with a quaint lodge in classical style. On the left, hidden by high hedges, is Hogg House, former home of Ralph Hogg, the reputed maker of the first iron cannon in the country. Walk down the avenue of magnificent trees and you come to the ancient church of Buxted (Old English 'place where beeches grow' – and they still do!)

Built in 1250 on the site of an earlier building, the rare dedication of the church refers to Margaret, wife of Malcolm III of Scotland, who was a daughter of the Saxon king of England, Edmund Ironside. Her daughter married Henry I of England and it is through her that the present Royal family traces its descent from Saxon kings. Much of the Buxted church goes back to Norman times and the booklet available in the church gives details of these. Of particular interest are the fine beams in the roof, the early figure of St Margaret over the east window and the 700 year-old vestment chest.

The church also has a connection with the Wealden iron industry: William Levett, the Rector of Buxted from 1533–45, had a 'servant', Ralph Hogg, to whom he entrusted the making of cannon, the first in England. He left him in his will money and six tons of 'sowes' or large iron bars. That Hogg prospered is evident from the large house he later built at the entrance to the park. There also survives a petition of his to Queen Elizabeth dated 1574 protesting against rumours that he had been selling cannon abroad. This document contains most valuable information about the industry at that time.

One wonders at the isolated situation of such an imposing church. The answer is twofold: it was the parish church of no fewer than seven present-day parishes including Uckfield. Secondly, the original Buxted village was built round the church. The site was examined by the Sussex Archaeological Society a few years ago and they found traces of the 'lost' village running east and west of the church. The line of the village streets can be traced in some places by a low ridge.

The original site of Buxted Place was adjacent to the church on the south side but after disastrous fires the mansion was rebuilt on its present site some distance further south.

The present large village of Buxted, with a railway station, shops, etc., is $\frac{3}{4}$ mile along the A272. The White Hart Inn serves meals and bar snacks every day except Sundays. The Post Office is open on weekdays except Wednesday afternoons.

Buxted Place

From the church, the path continues in the same direction; a sign guides you at first along the rhododendrons on the boundary of the grounds of the estate and then down the slope.

You will see another path branching off half-right down the incline. This is the path you take for a diversion to Uckfield (see page 156).

Hempstead Mill near Uckfield

At the junction with a path coming from the right, turn left, making for the estate cottage. Go past the cottage and sharp right, by a broken stile, along the (west) bank of the stream (do not go through the gate or over the footbridge). After about 300 m you pass through a high kissing-gate. Keep going, following the stream (the River Uck) flowing on your left. You pass some cottages and

Highlands Pond

emerge on to a road at the attractive Hempstead Mill. Turn left on the road, across the bridge over the river: immediately to your left is a stile and a waymark. The path then runs between fences for a short distance and over another stile. Turn half-right over the field, very soggy in wet weather, to a footbridge. From the bridge the path climbs to a stile and from this stile, round to the left of a silo and

Upton's Mill near the Wealdway between Buxted Park and Blackboys

other farm buildings – hardly an attractive area, this – and on to the
stile on your left at the top of the railway cutting. Go down the
steps, over the railway and up the other side. The path continues
half-left over the large field (there is a marker post) and into a small
thicket on to a country road, opposite Highlands pond, a favourite
spot for anglers.

Follow the road down the hill, crossing the stile at the bottom, on the right. This path follows the stream for some distance, over stiles and a footbridge, emerging on a road opposite a farm (the oast-house and buildings of Upton's Mill, 100 m southwards down the road make a delightful picture).

Go through the farmyard – likely to be very muddy in wet weather. The line of the path is not at all clear but runs parallel to the stream, across two fields (there is a stile). You eventually come out by the charming Tickerage Mill, said to be the site of a seventeenth-century furnace and forge. You turn right with the large, placid pond and the elegant house on your left.

Continue up the access road and through a gate. The path turns off on the right by the side of the house, Pippins, and crosses a field; a stile brings you to the B2102 on the outskirts of Blackboys.

Blackboys (Old English 'Blaca's Wood') is a pleasant village, most of it modern, although its earliest surviving mention is 1397. For the youth hostel, turn left from the stile on the B2102. At the crossroads a short distance further on, turn left and the hostel is 800 m down the road on the right. For the fifteenth-century Blackboys Inn turn right at the same crossroads: the inn is 400 m away on the corner of the B2192 Cross in Hand–Lewes road. Meals and bar meals are available every day including Sundays.

Route Northbound

You have reached the B2102 road on the outskirts of Blackboys*. Cross the road and in a few metres to the right there is a stile. From here the path crosses a field to a stile by a house, Pippins. Turn left down this metalled access road, go through a gate and at the bottom of the hill there is the attractive Tickerage Mill and placid pond – probably an early hammer-pond as there was a seventeenth-century furnace and forge at Tickerage. Cross the bridge over the stream, go past the building on the left and through the field gate. Turn left and from here for the next 1¼ miles the path runs through fields following the stream which for most of the way is on your left; but, after about ¾ mile, after you pass through a farmyard, the path follows along the other (south) bank. You eventually emerge on to a busy road, at the bottom of a hill. From the stile turn left up the quite steep rise; at the top of the rise, where the road bends, there is the large Highlands pond on the left. Opposite this pond is a stile and footpath sign. You go through a small copse and then half-left across a large field, the line of the path marked by a post. This leads to a stile above the deep railway cutting. Cross the railway by the steps and go up the other side.

You then follow the waymark on the second railway stile, bearing to the left, and, skirting the rather untidy farmyard, you will see two stiles leading down the slope to a footbridge over the stream at the bottom. Go over this footbridge bearing half-left – the line may not be clear – across the field, which is liable to be muddy in wet weather. This should bring you to a stile in the wire fence with the path running between two fences to another stile on the roadway. Turn right on the road, go over the bridge and you come to the attractive Hempstead Mill – deserving a picture or two.

Those who wish to make the diversion to Uckfield* can do so from here (see page 156).

Those not making the diversion, turn right between the mill and the adjacent building; follow the path along the river bank, through a high kissing-gate and on to a junction of paths (you are now in Buxted Park*). Turn left here, passing in front of the estate cottage, and then bear right up the slope. After a stile and a kissing-gate the path runs along the clump of rhododendrons – a sight in late spring – bordering the grounds of the estate. You pass the ancient church of St Margaret the Queen – with a fascinating history – and go down the avenue of magnificent trees, coming out on the A272 Buxted–Uckfield road.

The village of Buxted* is ¾ mile on the right (see page 147).

Turn left on the main road, down the hill, cross the river and the continuation of the Wealdway is on the right (concrete footpath sign) at the side of the entrance drive to Oast Farm and its farm shop. Keep straight on, following the hedge boundary of three fields, and go over two stiles to a kissing-gate by a garage, leading out onto the main A26 Uckfield–Crowborough road at Five Ash Down* (inn and Post Office Stores).

Cross over and opposite the garage is the footpath sign and waymark indicating the path, through gorse and bracken, across a couple of minor roads. Waymarks show the way by the left-hand side of a cottage and then straight over a field to the edge of a wood. The path descends on a clear track on the left from the stile through the wood (Hendall Wood). On emerging bear half-right across the next field towards the left-hand side of the cottage seen ahead. Go through the gateway in the centre of the field, making for the waymarked stile and gate in the far left-hand corner of the field. The path then follows between hedges to a stile and the driveway to Hendall Manor, a most attractive seventeenth-century farmhouse.

Turn left on the driveway, passing in front of the manor, bearing right, round the farm building, and then right by the side of the cottage. Go through the gate (with a waymark) and then turn left, along the field boundary to the gate at the edge of the wood (Furnace Wood*, belonging to the Forestry Commission).

The path drops down past a quarry (which may have been a source of iron-stone when the iron industry was in full swing). The waymarks on the trees at this spot are the most useful in helping you pick your way through the wood. Cross the wide track (or fire-break) at the bottom of the slope and carry on straight ahead along the forest track.

Cross the footbridge which you will see on the left, and almost immediately go over the stile on the right, the line of the path proceeding half-right across the field and over a footbridge to a gate on to the access road. Turn right from the stile and in a few metres, by the bend in the road, there is an Ashdown Forest waymark post (see page 132) pointing the way on the right through the bracken. This comes out on the outskirts of the village of Fairwarp* (turn left if you want the Foresters' Arms for refreshment or the Post Office).

Turn right along the road and in 450 m you reach a crossroads with the ornate iron gates to the private drive of Oldlands Park in front of you. Opposite the gates is Oldlands Corner, a charming house.

The 2000-year association of the Oldlands Estate* with the Wealden iron industry adds to the interest and attraction of this delightful spot.

At Oldlands Corner turn left with a tall holly hedge on your right – there is a 'Forest' waymark showing the line of the narrow path through the bracken and the special waymarks at strategic points help you find your way. After about 500 m keep a sharp lookout on your right for one of these waymark posts as there is a turn to the right of the path, up the slope (a lone birch tree which stands about 50 m beyond the turn in the path is a useful landmark).

You emerge on a very wide track. Turn left and you will notice a 'horse-head' bridle-way sign ahead of you. 160 m beyond this sign, on the right, is the waymark post showing the next stretch of the path through the bracken. The path crosses a private drive and then emerges on a metalled access road. Turn left down the road passing cottages and the handsome Brown's Brook Cottage on the right. The path then turns right over a footbridge and up through a wood.

At the end of the woodland path you cross the rear driveway of a white cottage. Go over this driveway, up the steep bank and then to the left round the cottage (there is a waymark post on the path here). Beyond the cottage the path rises gently through bracken, crossing an access track and eventually coming out by a bungalow. There is a stile and a waymark to the right of the bungalow, leading in a few metres to another stile on to a farm access road. Go straight along this road, through a gate outside a modern villa. The road bends to the right and on the left is a waymark post showing the continuation of the path. This leads through gorse and bracken to the highway on the south side of the large radio station whose tall masts dominate the scene. Bear left down the road. At the crossroads cross straight over and the waymark post will be seen. In a short distance you reach Camp Hill.

A few hundred metres down the main B2026 road from the cross-roads towards Uckfield is the café/teashop at Duddleswell.

Diversion

Uckfield. Walking mileage 2 miles (an extra 1½ miles)
Uckfield (Old English 'Ucca's field') is a good country shopping
centre but without any particular attraction. The shopping centre
lies along the main A22 London–Eastbourne road. There are a
number of dignified houses and buildings from the eighteenth
century and later: the parish church lies in a secluded corner a few
metres to the west of the main road and is worth a visit. The tower is
Norman but the rest of the building is early Victorian. In the High
Street the Maiden's Head Hotel is an attractive eighteenth-century
inn. The railway station at the bottom of the High Street provides
useful connections to Tunbridge Wells, Tonbridge and London.

Directions for southbound walkers
After passing Buxted church a footpath will be seen branching
half-right down the slope. This brings you to a footbridge leading to
a path through a wood. Keep straight on from the bridge through
the trees. This forest path will bring you to a newly-built residential
estate on the outskirts of Ukcfield, the line of the path continuing
through the estate, with the name of Tower Ride. At the top of the
rise the water tower is passed on your right and the right-of-way
keeps straight on as an asphalted footpath down to the main road in
Uckfield.
   To rejoin the Wealdway, at the main crossroads in the London
Road/High Street in Uckfield, opposite Church Road, is
Hempstead Road. ¾ mile down this road you come to Hempstead
Mill lying on the Wealdway.

Directions for northbound walkers
At Hempstead Mill (see page 153) keep straight on the road
(Hempstead Lane) for ¾ mile and this takes you to the centre of
Uckfield*. To rejoin the Wealdway, walk up the main London
Road and about 400 m north of the Church Road/Hempstead Road
crossroads, on the right, will be seen an asphalted footpath, Tower
Ride, with a signpost to Buxted. This pleasant path takes you past
the water tower above Uckfield, through a new housing estate and a

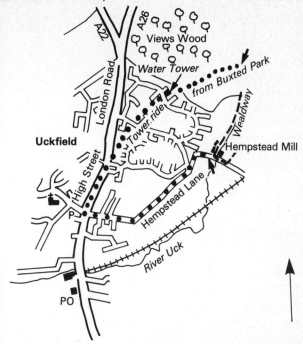

thick wood, Views Wood, into Buxted Park. Carry straight on from
the footbridge at the edge of the wood and up the slope. You can
see Buxted church to the left and the path leading to it. The church
is on the Wealdway.

Public transport

Ashdown Forest (Camp Hill)

Bus services Uckfield: SD 119, 149. Irregular and infrequent. (From
    Poundgate, 1¼ miles east of Camp Hill) Crowborough–
    Poundgate–Uckfield–Lewes–Brighton: SD 729. Weekdays,
    hourly; Sundays, two-hourly.

Uckfield

Five Ash Down

Bus services Crowborough–*Five Ash Down*–Uckfield–Lewes–
Brighton: SD 729. Weekdays, hourly; Sundays, two-hourly.

Uckfield

British Rail Crowborough, Edenbridge, Oxted, E. Croydon,
  London. Weekdays only, hourly.
Bus services Ashdown Forest (Camp Hill): SD 119, 149. Irregular
  and infrequent. Crowborough–Five Ash Down–*Uckfield*–Lewes–
  Brighton: SD 729. Weekdays, hourly; Sundays, two-hourly.
  Blackboys–Hellingly–Eastbourne: SD 190/1. Weekdays only,
  hourly.

Buxted

British Rail Uckfield–*Buxted*–Crowborough–Edenbridge–Oxted–E.
  Croydon–London. Weekdays only, hourly.
Bus services Camp Hill: SD 149. Tuesdays, Thurdays, Saturdays,
  a.m. and noon. Uckfield: SD 149. Weekdays only, a.m. and
  noon.

Blackboys

Bus services Uckfield–*Blackboys*–Hellingly–Eastbourne: SD 190/1.
  Weekdays only, hourly. Uckfield: SD 148/9. Weekdays only,
  noon. Brighton–Lewes–*Blackboys*–Ashford–Canterbury: SD
  718. Saturdays only, a.m. and p.m.

Note SD = Southdown. Service enquiries: telephone Brighton
  (0723) 606600.

Accommodation

Fairwarp (Ashdown Forest)

Romany Cottage	B&B.	On route.
Fairwarp	Evening meal.	Turn off foot-
Uckfield		bridge midway
E. Sussex TN22 3BL		Brown's Brook
Telephone Nutley (082571)		and Oldlands
2693		Corner.

Buxted

Heatherwode Farm	B&B.	$1\frac{1}{4}$ miles
Pound Green	Evening meal.	from route.
Buxted		
E. Sussex TW22 4JM		
Telephone Buxted (0825810)		
2131		

Blackboys

Youth Hostel	Members only	800 m from route.
Gun Road		
Blackboys		
Uckfield		
E. Sussex		
Telephone Framfield (082582)		
607		

Section 6

Blackboys to **Hellingly** 9½ miles

General description

From Blackboys to Hellingly you are on the Low Weald and the route of the Wealdway runs across fields and through patches of woodland; there are occasional rises in the ground, but nothing to match the heights of Ashdown Forest and the rest of the High Weald. The heathland has been left behind but this does not imply that you are now passing through a fertile and blossoming land. The soil is mostly clay and you may find some fields soggy after rain. The woods are pleasant and bright with bluebells and other wild flowers in spring and early summer. The fields you cross are mainly pasture and you do not see many crops being grown. A glance at a modern road map will confirm that this wide band of country that you are crossing is sparsely populated, with few villages. The writer of the informative and most interesting leaflet on sale in Chiddingly's church points out for example how few buildings there are in the village itself but that the parish of only 800 people includes many scattered 'settlements' all linked by 30 miles of footpath.

It looks as though the area was late in clearance and development, and difficulty in communications must have contributed to this: local names such a 'Foul Mile', 4 miles east of Chiddingly, are quite eloquent! Only in recent years have roads been reasonable. The iron industry brought work and wealth for about 300 years from the late fifteenth century and some of the lovely mediaeval houses were originally homes of the local iron-founders. The only foundry site actually on the Wealdway in this section is Newplace Farm where the house is comparatively modern, but there are some older ones not far from the path near Gun Hill, whose names obviously have a connection with the industry, as have Forge Wood and Smithland Wood nearby.

For those interested in ferreting out old iron-industry sites and splendid country manors a 3½ mile diversion is suggested (2 miles on a footpath and 1½ miles on a country road with fine views). The footpath takes in the site of Stream furnace and forge that were at work at least from 1548 to 1724; Stream Farm, the seventeenth-century home of the French family, owners of Stream for 100 years or more; and Stonehill, described by Pevsner as 'the perfect timber-framed Sussex house of the fifteenth century'. The Stream Mill could be the site of an earlier corn mill mentioned in the Domesday Book.

Although in the headings to our text we keep to 'northbound' and 'southbound', the route between Chiddingly and Gun Hill on this section is east-west. You have the advantage of some good views of the South Downs in clear weather.

As far as conditions are concerned, the way can occasionally be muddy in or after wet weather. There are probably more stiles to cross than on other sections but most are in good condition and should remain so. They did not provide the two septuagenarians who made this report with any difficulty!

Food is to be had at East Hoathly, Chiddingly, Gun Hill and Hellingly and accommodation at East Hoathly.

MAPS
OS 1:50 000 199
OS 1:25 000 TQ 42/52, 41/51

Route Southbound
Having reached the main B2102 road on the outskirts of Blackboys turn right from the stile and cross over. About 100 m down the road, on the left, is a stile with a waymark. Follow the path running close to the field edge on the right. Go over the next stile, turning left on the country road; in a few metres on the right is another waymarked stile showing the continuation of the path along the left-hand (east) boundary of the fields ahead. A gate with a footpath sign then indicates the way through a pleasant and extensive wood. You emerge on the approaches to farm buildings with, on your left, the landscaped gardens, shining lake and gracious mansion of Newplace Farm.

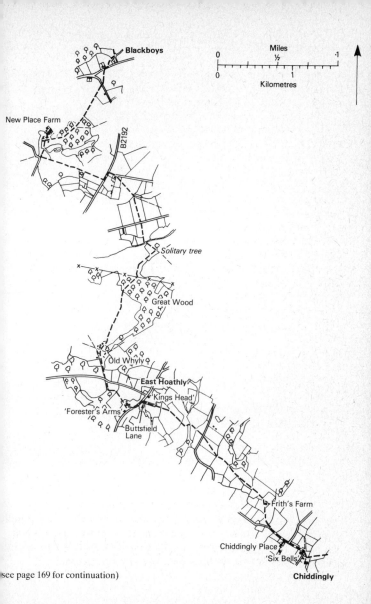

Blackboys

Miles

New Place Farm

B2192

Solitary tree

Great Wood

Old Whyly

East Hoathly

'Kings Head'

'Forester's Arms'

Buttsfield
Lane

Frith's Farm

Chiddingly Place

'Six Bells'

Chiddingly

(see page 169 for continuation)

Newplace Farm, near Blackboys

The lake and the wood give rise to the possibility of yet another link with the iron industry. A search in Straker's *Wealden Iron* confirms that large quantities of furnace cinder have been found on the site and 'the pond has every appearance of an iron pond'. No documentary evidence has apparently been discovered.

Passing through the farm and bearing left down the drive you will find, if you are fortunate enough to be walking in the spring, a breathtaking display of daffodils on either side: an unforgettable picture with the small stream tumbling from the lake over a miniature waterfall. The old wall of the drive and the trees in their spring finery complete the scene.

At the bottom of the drive turn left on the roadway, go over the bridge and cross the stile seen on the left, with its waymark. The line follows the fence of the wood on your left and then straight across in the same direction towards the left-hand (western) boundary of the small isolated copse seen ahead. On reaching the copse you will find that waymarks indicate the route from there: continue straight on, keeping the same direction, to a stile in a gap in the far hedge. This brings you to the main B2192 Lewes–Cross in Hand road. Bear left for 150 m and then right at the road junction, signposted to Waldron.

200 m along this road the Wealdway continues over the stile at the side of the bungalow with the name of Perrins. From here the path runs half-right towards a waymarked stile. From the stile the direction is across the next field down the slope, to the right. At the bottom of the slope you enter a bush-covered hollow with a rivulet running through. Go up the other side and you should find a stile with waymark. From here bear right, keeping parallel to the right-hand field boundary. You come out over a stile on a minor road.

Directly opposite the path continues parallel to the field hedge on the right and the power line down to another hollow with some trees. Here you cross a footbridge and make for a solitary oak tree in the centre of the field in front. At the tree, on which there is a waymark, turn sharp right towards a couple of stiles by some trees ahead of you. Cross the large field, keeping the same direction, heading for a wood on the crest of the slope and the entrance of the path shown by a white marker post. Follow this path through the wood – all that is left of Great Wood after a recent clearance – and you emerge on to a farm road after crossing a plank bridge over a ditch.

Descend towards the farm in the distance along the concrete road between fences and through the farm buildings, passing a public footpath sign. The farm or rather mansion, Old Whyly, is seen on the left. The drive, an avenue of fine trees, leads to the main A22 Eastbourne road.

It is fascinating to learn that the name Whyly of this obviously expensively renovated stud-farm marks one of only a very few places in the whole of Kent and Sussex whose origin could go back to pagan times, at least to 650 AD and possibly to pre-Roman times, as it is Celtic for 'the shrine of the idol'. Tacitus, the Roman historian of the first century AD, mentions that the 'Germans' built shrines to their gods in the middle of the forests: Whyly certainly had its 'Great Wood' covering the area in Celtic times.

Cross the road and directly opposite the continuation of the path will be seen. Follow this round the edge of the trees and you come out at the village school and the fine old church at East Hoathly, on the main A22 Eastbourne road.

East Hoathly (Old English 'heath-covered clearing') has some pleasing old dwellings, some on the Wealdway itself, and an imposing mediaeval church of which only the tower (sixteenth-century) remains, the rest being a Victorian restoration. The Pelham 'buckle' symbol decorating the doorway of the tower is of interest: the Pelhams were one of the great landowning families in East Sussex and the story is that the French King John II presented the buckle of his sword belt to a Pelham after his defeat at Poitiers in 1356. The 'buckle' is found in a number of places: Chiddingly is one, as we will see when we pass through. The Buckle Inn on the sea-front between Seaford and Newhaven is another reminder of the legend.

It was from a Pelham – as quoted in the chapter on background – that has come down to us what is probably the earliest letter in existence in the English language – Lady Joan Pelham's 'brave and beautiful' letter written in the fourteenth century to her husband.

The church is one of the few that is kept locked so unless you

East Hoathly

attend a service you cannot see the interior, with its unusual stained glass. An East Hoathly worthy, Thomas Turner, kept a diary for the years 1754–65 giving a unique account of Sussex village life in those days. Grocer, undertaker and teacher, his pious resolutions to eat and drink less, followed regularly by fits of remorse at having 'fallen', particularly for the drink, strike a modern chord. The comments on the journeys he had to make confirm that road conditions must have been atrocious. The diary, edited by F.M. Turner, should be available at local libraries, for those interested.

The Foresters' Arms, with food and accommodation, is on the right as you join the main road from the path. There is also the King's Head over the crossroads on the left. Meals and bar snacks are served daily including Sundays. There is a carpark near the church.

To continue the Wealdway, cross the A22, bear left and take the first turning on the right, Buttsfield Lane. Passing some pleasant houses and modern bungalows, the route continues through a 'squeeze' stile and ahead as a clear path, over stiles and through a small copse. From the copse keep straight on with field hedge on your left to a gate seen in front of you and then to a narrow country road. Cross over to the gate opposite (there is a footpath sign) and from there the line of the route is straight ahead. Cross sometimes damp fields, through gates, some of which are waymarked. You should emerge from the last field gate on to a concrete access road through Frith's Farm. Follow this (resplendent with daffodils in spring) past the farm and on to the motor road. Turn left and you soon see on the right Place Farm, the site of a famous mansion, Chiddingly Place. A few metres farther you come to the tiny centre of Chiddingly: Six Bells pub, village stores and beautiful church.

Chiddingly church (Old English 'Cedda's settlement') with its 40 m (130 ft) high stone spire – one of only three ancient churches in Sussex with a stone spire – is one of the best-known landmarks of the Weald. The walls of the tower on which the spire stands are 1.4 m ($4\frac{1}{2}$ ft) thick to enable them to bear the weight which they have done successfully for over 500 years, although there must have been a spasm of apprehension in 1897 when lightning damaged the tower. As a safeguard for the future a huge chain was fixed round the tower, as you can see.

In the interior of the church there is an impressive monument to Sir John Jefferay, one of Queen Elizabeth's high officials. It was his

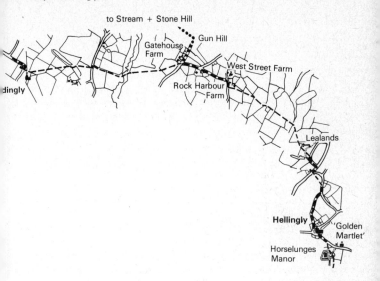

grandson who built Chiddingly Place, the site of which you passed
en route. The present farmhouse incorporates some of the original
Tudor buildings. One can make out what seems to be bricked-up
Tudor windows. Peter Brandon in his fine book, *The Sussex
Landscape*, mentions that this was the first E-shaped Elizabethan
mansion to be built in Sussex – Parham near Pulborough is the
best-preserved example in this style.

   The chancel of the church is Victorian but the pillars and arches
of the nave are from the fourteenth century or earlier. There are six
bells in the tower, the earliest of which is 350 years old. The Six
Bells pub, which itself goes back to 1774 reflects the close
connection there often was between church and pub. Bell-ringing is
thirsty work and no doubt Mine Host of the Six Bells was grateful
on many occasions to the bell-ringers for their regular support. At
Newdigate in Surrey the Six Bells pub certainly got its name from
the sixth bell that was added to Newdigate church tower in 1803.

Chiddingly Place, showing windows of the former Tudor mansion

Chiddingly figures in the Domesday Book and, although there was no church in pre-Conquest times, the mill that is mentioned is identified with Stream Mill, which you can visit on the suggested diversion.

The Six Bells in Chiddingly is open every day except Monday and serves bar snacks whenever it is open. It has an unusual collection of

Chiddingly village

old enamel advertising signs inside. The Post Office Stores is open on weekdays except Thursday afternoons.

Opposite the church is a stile with a footpath sign and waymark directing you diagonally across the field and on down the slope and over waymarked stiles to a stream in a small wood. On emerging from the wood make for the clump of gorse in the far left-hand corner of the field and you come to a minor road. Turn left and in a few metres on the right is a stile with a footpath sign. Follow the direction, parallel with the hedge on the left, to another footbridge over a small stream in a copse. A waymarked stile shows the route from here towards the left across the field where Gatehouse Farm will soon be seen ahead. A metal farm gate brings you out on the roadway. Turn left.

This is Gun Hill, a charming corner with old cottages and an oast house. Up the hill is the Gun Inn, a popular hostelry where meals and bar snacks are available daily in opening hours.

The name Gun Hill obviously refers to the manufacture of cannon locally, started in the mid-1500s. Stream Mill, ¾ mile by footpath to the west of Gun Hill, was a busy foundry run from the sixteenth century by the French family – they have their monument in Chiddingly church – and 2 miles to the north in Waldron cannon were definitely made. These massive weapons were taken by ox cart to the Ouse River, put on boats to the coast and then to wherever they were being installed: Chatham, Portsmouth and so on. Stonehill Farm near Stream Mill is said by Pevsner to be 'the perfect timber-framed Sussex home of the fifteenth century' and was probably lived in by one of the iron-founders. Stream Mill and Stonehill are visited on the suggested diversion (see page 178).

From Gatehouse Farm cross over at the T-junction and take the road signposted 'Coggers Cross'. A short way along the road, on the right, is a farm access road signed to West Street Farm and Rock Harbour Farm. The Wealdway route runs along this road, by a pond and bending to the right, first past West Street Farm and then Rock Harbour Farm. Immediately past the latter there is a gate and stile on the left; cross this stile and go on to the two stiles straight ahead. There are good views of the South Downs on your right if the weather is clear. Continue through a gate and on to where there are two more stiles at the edge of some trees and over one more stile, keeping the field edge on your right.

You then come to a wood: there is a stile on the right in the hedge

West Street Farm near Gun Hill

bordering the wood. Cross this stile and descend the slope to a
footbridge and a stile. Go up the incline on the other side and then
down anothe slope to a plank footbridge with a footpath sign.
Proceed towards the house, Lealands, on the crest of the next rise.
Go over the stile in the fence, and the line of the path passes round
the house and half-right over the next fence. Through the line of

Cottages surrounding Hellingly churchyard

trees, you emerge on an access road. Turn right and this brings you to the main A267 Horam–Eastbourne road.

Cross over at the T-junction; a few metres up the side road, on the right, are steps and a stile. The path then goes half-right up the rise in the field and comes out at a six-barred gate in the field boundary. From the gate turn right on this quiet road and in a few metres you come to the village of Hellingly with a grateful thought to the powers-that-be for having arranged for this charming spot to be bypassed so effectively.

There are some most attractive cottages and houses of varying ages and styles as you approach the churchyard – the Wealdway runs right through. The earliest surviving documentary mention of Hellingly (Old English 'clearing of the hill-dwellers') is in 1121 but the circular churchyard is unique and points to an earlier Saxon origin. The interesting booklet available in the church, besides describing the fascinating architectural features of the church representing many styles from the thirteenth century onwards, explains the background of the 'circular churchyard' theory. Apparently until about 750 AD burial customs followed those of the Romans, i.e. all burials had to take place outside the town or settlement, but at about that date the Pope gave general consent for burials close to the church. The early 'churchyards' were made circular following the traditional shape of the prehistoric barrows or burial mounds found in many places on the Downs nearby.

   A lovely feature of Hellingly churchyard are the old cottages, kept in immaculate condition, along the north rim. The church, the churchyard, the cottages and the flowering cherry tree in the centre make another unforgettable Wealdway picture in the spring. The fine timbered Horselunges Manor just south of the church is described in the next section. The Golden Martlet pub is a few metres east, beyond the bridge.

Route northbound

Take the road leading from the gate in the far left-hand (north west) corner of Hellingly* churchyard. You soon come to where there is a road junction. Keep to the left and in about 150 m, on the left, is a six-barred field gate with a waymark. The path runs half-right down the slope of the field and comes out over a stile and down some steps, lower down the road.

   At the T-junction with the A267 Eastbourne–Tunbridge Wells road, cross over. To the right is an access road with a sign to 'Lealands, Westenden Farm, Mt Pleasant'. Tale this road and, after passing a lodge, on the left is a stile. From this stile the route crosses a field, skirting the grounds of the large house, Lealands, with stiles over fences. Keep the same direction down the slope to a plank footbridge at the bottom. Go down into a hollow with trees, over another footbridge and up the other side to a stile in the hedge on the right. Turn left along the hedge and then continue straight on in the same direction, crossing a number of stiles and passing through one gate, until a final stile by the side of Rock Harbour Farm brings you to the farm access road. Turn right, passing firstly Rock Harbour Farm and then West Street Farm with its pond. You emerge on to a country road; turn left along this road and you shortly arrive at a T-junction with a pleasant converted oast house on the corner. Carry straight over to the other side of the road, and a little to the left beyond the entrance of Gatehouse Farm and its pond is a metal farm gate. (The hamlet is Gun Hill* and the Gun Inn is up the hill to your right.)

The direction from the farm gate is now half-left over the field down to a small stream. The tall spire of Chiddingly church can be seen ahead and used as a marker. Go through the copse and over the footbridge, the path following the field boundary on your right. You eventually come to a country road – turn left down the hill and in a few metres, on the other side of the road, is the stile with a footpath sign showing the way across a field down to a wood in the far corner and a footbridge. From the bridge the path continues in the same direction, almost due west, across three stiles, most of them adequately waymarked, until you reach Chiddingly*.

From Chiddingly, keep on the road past the church and Place Farm (formerly Chiddingly Place*). Turn right on the farm access road, you will see on your right the sign 'Frith's Farm'. Follow this road, passing the farm buildings and the trim farmhouse to a field gate. From here, although the line might not be clear on the ground, the path carries on almost straight ahead, following at first a line of hedge and small trees to another field gate (it is often muddy here). About ¾ mile from the farm gate and after two more gates a country road is reached. Immediately opposite there is a bridleway-sign, the route proceeding along the hedge on the right, entering a small copse. On emerging from the copse keep the field boundary on your right. Where the path forks, take the left fork; finally you come to a 'squeeze' gate and a roadway lined mostly with modern houses, and emerge on to the A22 Eastbourne Road at East Hoathly*.

Turn left and cross over. (The Foresters' Arms with food and accommodation is a short way further down the main road on the left.) Take the road on the right, Church Marks Lane, then go through the churchyard and along the asphalted path with the village school on your left. Follow the footpath where it bears left round a spinney and through a gate on to the main A22 road.

Cross over and take the access road opposite running between an avenue of trees. Bear right past a public footpath sign through the buildings of Old Whyly Farm*. Another footpath sign shows the way ahead on a concrete farm road between fences. At the top of the rise, where the road bears to the left, keep straight on and eventually cross a plank footbridge into the wood, Great Wood.

At the far edge of Great Wood make for two stiles seen by a few trees down the slope. The farm silos in the distance are good markers for the direction needed. From the stiles the line of the path is to the solitary tree in the field ahead. At the tree turn sharp left down to the gully with trees and a plank bridge. Up the other side of the gully and keeping parallel to the hedge on the left you should find a stile on a narrow country road at the top of the rise.

Cross to the waymarked stile opposite and go straight ahead, parallel to the hedge on the right, down to a bush-filled hollow and small stream. Go over the stile on the other side and then half-left across the field to yet another stile and on to a country road by the side of a bungalow. Bear left on this road and on to the T-junction with the B2192 Lewes–Cross in Hand main road.

Turn left on the main road and cross over. In 150 m on the right are steps and a stile with a yellow waymark. From this stile the line of the path goes across the large field to the right-hand (northern) edge of the small spinney seen ahead to your left. Continue in the same direction, the route running finally alongside the fence of the grounds of Newplace Farm* and down to the road by a stile. Turn right, cross the bridge and bear right up the drive signed 'Newplace Farm'. This entrance is flanked in the spring with hundreds of daffodils – a lovely sight. Follow the drive where it bends to the right through the farm buildings, with the dignified mansion, landscaped garden and lake to your right.

The path continues through Newplace Wood – bluebell-covered in spring – and then across fields and over stiles, all waymarked, to a roadway. Turn left and then right in 100m over the stile by the side of the house Peddlers. Keep to the field edge on your left and you emerge on to the B2102 on the outskirts of Blackboys.

Diversion

Stream Mill, Stream Farm and Stonehill (3½ miles circular walk).

Directions for south- and northbound walkers
This diversion takes you past Stream Mill, an important medieval iron-foundry and the seventeenth-century Stream Farm. Stonehill is one of Sussex's finest timbered houses. From Gatehouse Farm (pages 172 and 176), instead of taking the road signed 'Coggers Cross', continue up the hill to the Gun Inn. Take the bridle-way opposite bearing the sign 'Strood Farm'. This dips down between high banks to Strood Farm; continue straight on past the converted dwellings on your left. The route then bears left round a patch of woodland and comes out on a narrow country road by the side of a house.

Cross the road and in the field gap opposite is a concrete footpath sign. Bear half-right (due north) crossing the large field diagonally. You will see a wide gap in the boundary hedge to the left in the far corner of the field. Go through this gap and straight ahead towards the woodland on the far side of the field. On the edge of the wood is another gap through which a clear path leads through the wood, emerging by some houses. The path passes along the front of the first house. You have to negotiate a plain wire fence to join a wide farm access track. Turn left on to the track.

The group of dwellings on the left were formerly the buildings of Stream Mill, a furnace and iron foundry that was in operation for 400 years up to 1725. The buildings have been converted into normal dwelling houses and there is little trace of the mill although the smallest of the houses is obviously a mill-house and, just

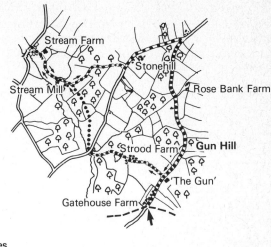

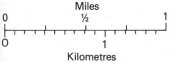

beyond, a mill-race runs under a bridge over the farm track.
Looking down from the bridge it will be seen that square blocks of
stone have been used to line the pool below the mill-race. There was
a large mill-pond behind Stream Mill but this became choked with
weed and has disappeared. A short time ago a piece of iron 3.35 m
long was dug up behind the Mill. This turned out to be a
seventeenth-century boring bar used for making the barrels of
cannon, providing ample proof of the part played by Stream Mill in
the manufacture of these huge weapons. The boring bar is
preserved in the Sussex Archaeological Society's museum at Anne
of Cleves House in Lewes.

    Some experts say that the mill is on the site of one mentioned in
the Domesday Book (it would have been a grain mill, of course) so
there could have been a mill here of one kind or another for 800

years. Stream Mill is mentioned in a number of old documents. In one dated 1548 a Royal Commission recommended that a number of Sussex iron-works should be suppressed, including 'the iron hammer of Chiddingly' – this was the Stream forge – as they used so much timber for fuel that coastal towns such as Rye and Hastings, as well as our possessions at that time on the French coast such as Calais, had insufficent for their requirements. No action was apparently taken to put the recommendations into effect.

Proceed straight on through the wood, the path emerging at the outbuildings of Stream Farm. Pass through the farmyard to the roadway. On the left is the impressive seventeenth-century Stream Farm itself, former home of the French family, wealthy landowners and iron-founders.

If you turn left down the narrow road to the bridge you will see in the stream the remains of stonework placed there to strengthen the banks and also the orange-coloured iron stain at the river bottom.

After having absorbed the sturdy country architecture of Stream Farm and admired its flowerbeds and trim lawn with the curious little brick summerhouse, retrace your steps back through the farmyard to Stream Mill. At the mill keep on the wide bridle-way track that curves away to the left, eventually entering the wood, Forge Wood. It is evident that this workmanlike track has seen the passage of heavier loads than hay or turnips: huge cannon and other products of the forge.

Where the track comes out on the road turn left and in a few metres, on the right, you can look through the bars of the lovely iron gates of Stonehill – Pevsner's 'perfect timbered Sussex house'. The fifteenth-century features have been lovingly restored and those with cameras will be able to record one of the little-known gems of the county.

To make your way back to Gun Hill, continue up the road until you come to a fork. Take the turning signposted 'Gun Hill 1¼ miles'. Although on a road this is a pleasant walk; at one spot on the right there is a marvellous view over the Weald with Chiddingly church spire presiding in the distance over acres of tree and pasture. At the bottom of Gun Hill is the road to Coggers Cross (for southbound walkers) and, on the right, past Gatehouse Farm, the path for northbound walkers.

Public transport

Blackboys

Bus services Uckfield–*Blackboys*–Hellingly–Eastbourne: SD 190/1.
  Weekdays only, hourly. Uckfield: SD 148/9. Weekdays only,
  noon. Brighton–Lewes–*Blackboys*–Ashford–Canterbury: SD
  718. Saturdays only, a.m. and p.m.

East Hoathly

Bus services E. Grinstead–Uckfield–*East Hoathly*–Horsebridge–
  Eastbourne: SD 780. Weekdays only, approx. two-hourly.
  Hailsham–Horsebridge–*East Hoathly*–Uckfield: SD 180.
  Weekdays only, a.m. and p.m. (Saturdays not p.m.).

Hellingly (Village Hall)

Bus services Eastbourne–Horsebridge–*Hellingly*–Heathfield: SD
  190/1. Weekdays, hourly; Sundays, two-hourly.

Note SD = Southdown. Service enquiries: telephone Brighton
  (0723) 606600.

Accommodation

Blackboys See Section 5.

East Hoathly

Foresters' Arms	B&B. On route.
East Hoathly	Evening meal
Uckfield	except Thursday.
E. Sussex	
Telephone Halland (082584)	
208	

Section 7

Hellingly to **Wilmington** 8 miles

General description

This section, shorter than the previous ones, has much of interest to reveal. The going is good but liable to be muddy in parts if there has been rain about. There are no real gradients as you are in the 'flatlands' between the Weald and the South Downs. You are not yet in the pure chalk until you get to Wilmington itself – you cross a strip of 'greensand' that runs for 30 miles along the foot of the Downs from the Channel to the River Arun. The Romans took advantage of this greensand to build cross-country roads to connect the sea base at Pevensey with Stane Street running north from Chichester: the Wealdway crosses one of these south of Arlington. Most of the early settlements have their origin after the Romans left, from the Saxon invaders who penetrated inland up the rivers, in this case the most easterly, the Cuckmere.

After the Conquest the Church was quick to secure good sites on this comparatively fertile ground and on the Wealdway are Michelham Priory and Wilmington Priory, both open to the public except in the winter. The two priories belong to the Sussex Archaeological Trust and great care has been taken to explain the layout of the buildings and the life of the monks. Those with cameras will find plenty to record. There were nearly 70 monastic establishments in pre-Reformation Sussex, and Michelham and Wilmington are two of the eleven of which there are any remains to be seen. One can appreciate the important parts they must have played in the life of the county in the Middle Ages. They served the community in many fields: in husbandry, charity and scholarship, for example, as those who have seen the fascinating exhibition at Beaulieu Abbey in Hampshire will appreciate; but after the Black Death in the middle of the fourteenth century, decline set in. This and their prior allegiance to the Pope made their abolition inevitable. Many of the fine houses seen on this and other parts of

Miles
0   ½   1

0   1
Kilometres

Hellingly
Horselunges Manor

Mill   A271

to Lewes

River Cuckmere

Upper Horsebridge

A22

Hempstead Farm

Upper Dicker
to Lower Dicker

'Plough Inn'   PO

to Berwick

PO

Parkwood Farm

Mickleham Priory

R. Cuckmere

Park pale
Barn

Arlington
'Yew Tree Inn'

Arlington Reservoir

Stapley's

Line of Roman Road

River Cuckmere

Milton Gate
to Lewes

A27   Crossways Hotel
to Eastbourne →

'Wilmington Arms'

Wilmington Priory   **Wilmington**

the Wealdway were built on former monastic sites by the new Tudor generation of the rich and the powerful.

A gem in this area is the church of Arlington, built possibly on a Roman site but definitely going back to Saxon times.

It is not only in historical associations that this section of the path is rich. Two of my lasting memories are having the opportunity to record the song of a nightingale at 3 o'clock in the afternoon near Arlington, and seeing the profusion of bluebells in a small wood near Upper Dicker where 'a carpet' was the only possible description.

There are an adequate number of pubs *en route* where meals or refreshments are available.

Details of a suggested diversion from Wilmington to Alfriston are given at the end of the next section.

MAPS
OS 1:50 000 199
OS 1:25 000 TQ 41/51, 40/50

Route southbound
From the south gate of Hellingly churchyard take the road straight ahead. A few metres down this road is the bridge over the Cuckmere River. Just beyond the river, on the right, is a kissing-gate to the path, leading across a field to another kissing-gate. Keep straight on, parallel to the moat on your right, until you come to the private drive of Horselunges Manor. Cross straight over the drive.

Horselunges Manor is another famous Sussex manor house. Built in the late fourteenth century it is an early example of the breakaway from the usual fourteenth-century dwelling. In place of the 'great hall' stretching from floor to roof as the main living room, Horselunges was built with two storeys providing a large chamber over the 'hall' below. The type of house is known as 'continuous jetty' – the floor of the upper storey overhangs the front of the rooms below. The house has been carefully restored and with its moat – a rare feature – makes a splendid picture. The house is not open to the public.

Horsebridge Mill

After crossing the private drive the path continues between the garages and outbuildings of the manor to a field gate and kissing-gate. From there the path runs parallel with a draining ditch of the Cuckmere which flows invisibly a short distance away on the right. The path and river converge just above the mill at Horsebridge, the path running between the mill buildings and under the arch to the A271 which runs from the A22 Eastbourne road to Bexhill. Cross straight over at the T-junction opposite and go down the B3104. In a few metres, on the right, is a narrow metalled drive (at the time of writing with no sign or waymark) with a hedge on one side and a wooden fence on the other, leading behind houses on its right. Turn left off the drive in a few metres when reaching some cupressus trees and make for the passageway between fences seen on the left running behind gardens of a recently built estate. This leads to a field gate. Go through the gate and continue in the same direction.

The path eventually makes a little 'kink' to the right over a culvert and an iron gate; from here aim for the right boundary of the farm buildings visible in the distance across the large field. You come to a stile and then turn half-left, parallel to the fence of the farm buildings, to a stile with a signpost on the main A22 Eastbourne road.

Cross straight over the main road to a stile with a path leading half-right along a field edge. Turn sharp left at a waymarked field gate. The path from here goes straight for 500 m with the farm, Hempstead Farm, on your left. From the next stile for 700 m the route keeps to the boundary of several fields: first with the boundary on the right then, at a signpost, to the left of the field edge. At the next signpost you take the direction indicated across a small field to a footbridge and stile. From here ahead of you is a large field, inadequately marked, which could be ploughed up (as could some of the others); the best guidance one could give is to bear half-right in a south-west direction across this field aiming to the left of the bottom of the shallow 'V' made by the patches of woodland ahead.

You should find a waymarked stile with the path continuing diagonally half-left down the slope of a field. Turn left through a gap in the hedge boundary and you will come to a gate and stile, with a footpath sign, on the right. The path then runs parallel with the Cuckmere River to your left.

In the trees on the other side of the river will be seen Michelham Priory, surrounded by a moat. The site was in a natural bend in the Cuckmere. Cuts were made in the thirteenth and fourteenth centuries to complete the moat.

The fourteenth-century gatehouse of Michelham Priory

Cross the brick bridge over the Cuckmere on your left and then a second one over the moat; go through a gate. A few metres up the farm track a signposted stile will be seen on the right. From this stile the path runs diagonally across the field to a double stile seen in a gap in the hedge ahead.

Those wishing to visit Michelham Priory should turn sharp left from this double stile along the field path hugging the edge of the field. In about 50 m you come out on a roadway. Turn left and the entrance to the priory is 200 m down the road on the left.

The priory was founded in 1229 by Gilbert de l'Aigle, overlord of the Rape (district) of Pevensey, for thirteen Augustinian canons – Austin Friars in the City of London was a similar foundation. The Augustinians were the oldest of religious orders having been founded in 390 AD by Augustine of Hippo, that pleasure-loving Roman youth who became one of the greatest figures of Christendom.

The ravages of the Black Death (1348–9) hit the priory hard: more than half of the friars died and the devastation of the surrounding country must have been terrible. The priory went into decline: a 'visitation' ordered by the Archbishop in the 1400s found the friars guilty of many misdemeanours including unauthorised visits to the inn at the gate (was this the precedessor of the Plough?) and returning the worse for wear.

The priory was suppressed by Henry VIII in 1536 and most of the mediaeval building dismantled. Parts however were incorporated in the gracious Tudor residence built on the site by Henry Pelham (here again the Pelhams appear on the Wealdway) which is the chief feature of the present-day Michelham Priory. The north wall of the present house is the south cloister wall of the old priory, and the vaulted entrance hall and Prior's Room above are thirteenth-century – nearly 800 years old. The impressive and beautiful 18 m (60 ft) high Gateway House is fourteenth-century and is largely as it was when it was built. Its walls are 1.2 m (4 ft) thick, of local greensand stone on the outside with chalk and flint inside. The huge Tudor barn in the grounds is fascinating, and you can see marked out on the lawns the outline of the original priory and church buildings.

The house contains what must be a priceless collection of pictures and furniture illustrating the life of the priory and of the Tudor and later residents. The working mill in the grounds dates from the fifteenth and sixteenth centuries. To regain the Wealdway turn right out of the priory entrance; the road will bring you to Upper Dicker where you turn left at the crossroads.

Many absorbing details and further information are given in the admirable booklet obtainable at the priory. The priory is open to the public from mid-April to mid-October, daily, 11 a.m.–5.30 p.m. (closed 1–2 p.m.). Telephone: Hailsham 844224. Meals and refreshments are available.

From the double stile cross the field diagonally on a bearing north-west; nearing the line of buildings ahead, the path finishes alongside a fence and between two buildings (the one on the right is the Post Office Stores) and emerges into the B2108 road at Upper Dicker.

The earliest surviving mention of Dicker is in 1261 but the main influence in the growth of Upper Dicker (Lower Dicker, 1 mile to the north, is quite a separate hamlet) has been its association with Michelham Priory. Probably the 30 or so civilian employees of the priory lived in the village, as did those who supplied goods, utensils and those food items not produced by the friars. The large St Bede's School in the main road used to be the home in the early 1920s of Horatio Bottomley, one of the best-known figures of contemporary London. He was the founder of the magazine, *John Bull*, which had an enormous circulation. He fell foul of the authorities eventually but was a popular figure in the Dickers, distributing 'fivers' wholesale when he was 'in the money'. The Plough Inn serves meals and bar snacks daily.

Turn left down the B2108 and on the left-hand side, just past the Plough Inn, is a waymarked stile indicating the continuation of the Wealdway. Make for the stile seen in front of you and then across the large field parallel to the hedge on the right. You come to another stile on the edge of a small wood. The path runs along the right-hand (western) edge of the wood – a blaze of colour from the bluebells when I passed by in April.

On reaching a farm access road, turn left and, on the right in a few metres, is a stile and footpath sign. Cross the field to the gate ahead and from there aim slightly left down the slope. Go over another stile and a footbridge and you then emerge on to a large field on the banks of the Cuckmere. The official line is straight ahead, keeping the river some metres to your left, but if you wish you can walk along the bank of the twisting stream. There is always something of interest to see by the river if you watch out. The spire of Arlington church can be seen from the path.

It was from a small clump of brushwood on the other side of the river, occupying the site of an old moat, that I heard and took a recording of a nightingale singing at 3 o'clock in the afternoon: an ambition of years fulfilled!

A gate, a footbridge and a stile bring you to an unmetalled farm access road leading, to the left, to a long white-painted footbridge over the Cuckmere, shown on the map as Sessingham Bridge, named from the farm up the road. A short distance from the bridge, on the right, is a stile in the hedge.

The farm access road that crosses Sessingham Bridge is the south boundary of Michelham Priory deer park. Peter Brandon in *The Sussex Landscape* points out that about 150 m farther up the lane (past the stile) you can see clearly the 'park pale', the earthen bank that, surmounted by a paling or other type of fence, used to protect the deer park from intruders or prevent the deer from escaping. That it was not too successful is evident from records of the priory of many poaching cases. You can see the vestiges of the bank for about 800 m. The lane actually comes out on to a road opposite the extensive Abbot's Wood, obviously a former part of the deer park. All this shows the extent of the domains of a mediaeval monastery. They also had, of course, an income from various properties left them by pious benefactors.

From the stile a few metres up from Sessingham Bridge on the right, the path leads towards the right-hand side of a barn on the crest of the slope. To the right of the red barn there is a stile, the path proceeding along the left-hand edge of the next field. At the end of the field a series of well-marked stiles and a footbridge bring you through a spinney into Arlington churchyard.

Arlington church

Arlington (Old English 'homestead of the Earl's people') may be a 2000 year-old settlement. Brandon's book *The Sussex Landscape* mentions that the base of a Roman arch has been found under the chancel of the church and there are Roman bricks and tiles in the fabric. It could have been built on a Roman site – perhaps a Roman Christian temple. The present church is itself very old: the informative little leaflet in the church will tell you where to look for Saxon features. No part of the church is less than 450 years old. What intrigued me most were the heads of the Black Prince's parents, Edward III (1327–77) and his Queen, on the east window of the chancel, and the quote from the register of 1692 of a gift of £1.2s.0d. (worth 50 times as much nowadays) from this tiny community for the 'freeing of slaves in Turkey and Shajear (Sharjar) and suchlike places'. Christian Aid is obviously not a recent movement!

The Yew Tree inn is a short distance down the road to the left. Meals and bar snacks are available daily including Sundays.

The route goes across the churchyard to the roadway. Turn right past Benedict's Cottage to a stile and footpath sign.

In a short distance on the right there is a sign to Arlington Reservoir about 500 m away. You can walk around most of its perimeter but not always close to the water's edge. It is a good spot for watching waterfowl in spring and autumn.

The path bears left to a footbridge and stile, then goes straight ahead, over what is often boggy ground. Make for the right-hand (western) fence of the farm seen in front of you. Two stiles bring you out on to a metalled access road serving the waterworks houses. This in turn leads to a gate and stile on a roadway.

For those interested, this stretch of road is on the line of a Roman road from Pevensey via Polegate to Selmeston researched by I.D. Margary (Roman Ways in the Weald). If you turn left on this road, where it turns sharp left in a few metres a byway signed 'Alfriston' continues straight on. This is the line of the Roman road, seen to better advantage if you walk 100 m or so along it.

Cross the roadway opposite the access road; the Wealdway carries on down the bank and along the Cuckmere, then turns sharp left along a hedge and ditch until you reach a double stile. Turn right and go over the rise keeping to the line of the hedge on your right and passing the farm on the left. From the rise, go down to the dip, over a ditch and through a waymarked gate to a farm track, crossing the railway. The line of the route from the railway should be clear: go along the field edge until you bear right through two farm gates and through farm buildings to the A27 Lewes–Polegate road by a bus stop and shelter.

Cross the A27 and go down the minor road signed 'Milton Street ¾ mile'. 150 m along this road, on the left, by the house Sundown is a 'squeeze' gate and signpost 'Wilmington ½ mile'. This path leads straight across fields and over stiles; as you near Wilmington you cross to the south side of the ditch then along by a garden fence, emerging on to a roadway, past bungalows, to the road in the village of Wilmington.

Wilmington (Old English 'Willa's hill-meadow') is of Saxon origin and the estate is mentioned in the Domesday Book. It became the property of the Abbey of Grestain in Normandy, the monks founding the church to be the headquarters for the area, with a few monks in residence. The church and the living quarters formed together the Priory of Wilmington. What we see now is the ruined fourteenth-century Great Hall and other parts of the priory or house where the monks lived.

There is actually a greater proportion of ancient building on view in Wilmington Priory than there is at nearby Michelham Priory. The adjacent church has also much to show: there is architecture from every century from the twelfth to the sixteenth, as well as recent renovations. One feature of unique interest in the church is the fifteenth-century Butterfly Window in the North Chapel. The butterflies shown include the Camberwell Beauty, very rare in Britain nowadays, and the Apollo, which has probably never been seen here, showing that the artist was in all likelihood foreign. The booklet on sale in the church gives the key to the butterflies.

You can see you are no longer on Wealden clay. The church and priory and most of the village dwellings are built of flints, so easily extracted from the chalk of the Downs. Imported stone from outside the area was brought in for parts of the church where greater strength than the chalk could give was needed.

Wilmington village

Wilmington as a village no longer exists. There are no shops nor Post Office and even the former old village pub, the Black Horse, is now a dwelling house. Luckily, near the junction with the A27 you have the Wilmington Arms, a modern and helpful substitute for the Black Horse. Meals and bar snacks are available daily. The village street fortunately retains its character and is most pleasing to the eye. There is a free carpark at the far (south) end of the village street. From the end of the street the famous figure of the Long Man of Wilmington will be seen carved on the Downs (see the next section).

The priory is open to the public from mid-March to the end of October, on weekdays except Tuesdays from 10 a.m.–6 p.m.; Sundays 2–5 p.m. Telephone Alfriston (0323) 870537.

Route northbound

From Wilmington's village street the Wealdway takes the path on the left by the telephone kiosk. There is a concrete footpath sign by the side road, leading past trim bungalows to a path alongside a garden fence into fields beyond. This crosses over to the north bank of a ditch in a few metres and from there continues clearly across fields and over stiles to a minor road branching off the main A27 Polegate–Lewes road. Turn right from the 'squeeze' gate at the end of the path. On reaching the A27 cross straight over and take the farm access road opposite, to the right of the bus shelter.

Proceed through the farmyard gates to the left and then bear left taking the field path which, after crossing a ditch, continues northwards along the ditch and field boundary on your right. Stiles and a culvert take you over the railway. From the other side of the railway follow at first the wide farm track ahead as far as a waymarked gate and culvert. Here you leave the track to climb the rise on the left, leaving the farm on your right. At the bottom of the dip on the other side of the rise cross the double stile and turn left along the hedgerow and then to the right along the River Cuckmere. Follow the river bank and when you come to a roadway, cross straight over.

This roadway is along the line of a Roman road from Pevensey to Selmeston*.

The route continues over the stile by the side of the entrance gate to the waterworks. There is a sign to Arlington church. Take the metalled drive as far as the farm where there is a stile and sign 'to

Arlington village'. Go over this stile and make for Arlington church*
which can be seen ahead of you, over what is often boggy ground,
crossing two stiles and a footbridge.

If you wish to visit Arlington Reservoir about 500 m to your left,
follow the path that branches off to the left of our route, as
indicated by a footpath sign as you near the church.

Near the church there is a stile and signpost on your right, and the
route turns left through the churchyard from the short length of
roadway and leads to a path in the far left-hand corner of the
churchyard among the trees. Carry on over a footbridge to the left
and over well-marked stiles which bring you to a northbound path
with a barn on your left. Keep straight on with the field hedge on
your right, and at the end of the field go over the stile in the corner
by another barn. From this stile descend the slope towards two
small white posts; you will find the next stile a little to the right of
these.
    Turn left along the track leading to a long white footbridge over
the Cuckmere, Sessingham Bridge.

The track is the south boundary of the Michelham Priory deer
park*. The earth bank of the former 'park pale' can be seen farther
up the path to the right for those interested.

After crossing the bridge, turn sharp right over the stile and
footbridge and go through a gate. The line of the path from here
proceeds northwards a short distance to the left of the river but you
can if you wish follow the bank of the twisting course. The path
eventually crosses, by a footbridge, a ditch draining into the
Cuckmere and from there proceeds ahead to a field gate and across
another field in the direction of a house in the distance.
    On reaching the stile by this house turn left on the farm access
road and immediately sharp right over another stile from where the
path leads along the edge of a small wood – a mass of bluebells in
April – to a stile. Cross the next field keeping towards the boundary
on your left; go over yet two more stiles and you come out on the

B2108 road at Upper Dicker* opposite the Plough Inn (meals and bar snacks). Carry on up the road until you reach the Post Office Stores on the right.

Those wanting to visit Michelham Priory* should take the first turning on the right from the stile; the entrance to the priory is 800 m down this road. After visiting the priory return along this road for 200 m and take the footpath on the right which leads alongside a field to the double stile on the Wealdway route, as mentioned on page 187.

At the right-hand side of the Post Office Stores is a passageway between the houses. The Wealdway continues down this and out into the fields beyond. Keep straight on in the same direction and when you are over the slight rise ahead make for the far corner of the large field to a double stile. Continue across the field diagonally from the double stile to a stile on the farm road. Turn left and go through the metal gate and over two brick bridges, one over the priory moat and the other over the Cuckmere.

Turn right from the bridges, the path running parallel to the river on your right. Go over the signposted stile by a field gate, turning sharp left along the field boundary. Continue through the gap ahead and then half-right diagonally up the slope to a waymarked stile in the far corner. From here the line may be difficult to judge (the field may be ploughed or sown with crops). The direction is north-east: you can aim for the left-hand tree of the line of taller trees seen in the distance (they are poplars but not Lombardy poplars). The next stile is well hidden in the bushes near this left-hand tree.

From this stile, go over a footbridge and half-right across the small field to a signpost and stile in the far fence. From here the path keeps to the field edge, at first to the left of the boundary and then, at another signpost and stile, to the right of the boundaries of the next fields. Eventually you come to a straight path about 500 m long on the top of the rise with the farm, Hempstead Farm, to your right. After a stile and gate at the end of this stretch you turn sharp right towards the main A22 Eastbourne road seen ahead of you.

Cross straight over the A22 and a stile in the fence will be seen

opposite. The path from the stile runs parallel to the farm fence to
your right. Go over another stile and a footbridge, bearing half-right
across the large field and making for the end of a row of houses.
You cross two ditches and go through a gate, the line then following
the back fences of the houses to another field gate. The path
narrows between two fences and comes out on the approach to a
recently built estate. Continue to the clump of cupressus trees and
then turn right down a metalled access track between fences and out
on to the B2104 road.

   Turn left and cross over at the T-junction with the A271 road.
Through the arch opposite the path runs between the mill buildings
and bears left beside a garage. Follow the field path along the small
tributary stream of the Cuckmere until you reach a kissing-gate on
the boundary of Horselunges Manor*. Continue between the farm
buildings and cross the drive of the manor. The path runs over the
grass, parallel with the moat to your left, through another
kissing-gate, on the road. Turn left on this road (the Golden Martlet
pub is to the right), go over the bridge and you arrive at Hellingly*
church.

Public transport

Hellingly (Village Hall)

Bus services Eastbourne–Horsebridge–Hellingly–Heathfield: SD
   190/1. Weekdays, hourly; Sundays, two-hourly.

Horsebridge

Bus services E. Grinstead–Uckfield–E. Hoathly–*Horsebridge*–
   Eastbourne: SD 780. Weekdays only, approx. two-hourly.
   Hailsham–*Horsebridge*–E. Hoathly–Uckfield: SD 180.
   Weekdays only, a.m. and p.m. (Saturdays not p.m.). Eastbourne–
   Horsebridge–Hellingly–Heathfield: SD 190/1. Weekly, hourly;
   Sundays, two-hourly.

Wilmington

Bus services Eastbourne–Polegate–*Wilmington*–Alfriston–Seaford:
SD 126. Daily, two-hourly.

Note SD = Southdown. Service enquiries: telephone Brighton
(0723) 606600.

Accommodation

Upper Dicker

Mrs J. Head	B&B.	On route.
3 Crossways Cottages	Evening meal at	
Camberlot Road	Plough nearby	
Upper Dicker		
Hailsham		
E. Sussex BN27 3QG		
Telephone Hailsham (0323)		
843577		

Wilmington

Crossways Hotel	B&B.	On route.
Wilmington	Evening meal at	
Nr. Polegate	Wilmington Arms	
E. Sussex BN26 5SG	nearby.	
Telephone Polegate (03212)		
2455		

Wilmington to **Eastbourne** (East Dean road, A259) 7 miles

General description

For southbound walkers this is the 'home straight'. It is always good
to end an enterprise on a high note and this certainly describes the
7-mile walk over the South Downs. The sense of exhilaration and
freedom that comes from having left behind the busy world far
below you is increased by the marvellous views of the countryside –
the expanse of the Weald you have just crossed and the rolling
Downs behind and before you.

   Although most of the section is open downland the two hamlets
encountered, Folkington and Jevington, both have charm and
interest, particularly Jevington with associations as far back as the
Romans. Even more impressive, although you may need a practised
eye to detect the traces on the ground, is Combe Hill, on the route
above Jevington, where there are traces of a Neolithic (New Stone
Age) 'causewayed camp'. According to the experts, these camps
were not defensive but were connected with the daily life of the
tribe. They were most likely to have been 'corrals' for livestock,
having concentric rings of low embankments with many entrances.
The builders of such camps are thought to have been the first
'civilised' inhabitants of Britain. Unlike primitive man, they did not
depend on hunting for a livelihood but kept herds of cattle, pigs and
sheep and had learned to grow crops – a 'grain rubber' was found at
Combe Hill.

   From fragments of pottery found on the site it has been estimated
that the settlement dates from about 2500 BC and is therefore 4500
years old. Those interested will find more fascinating detail in
Gordon Copley's *An Archaeology of South-East England*.

   There is also, of course, the mysterious figure of the Long Man of
Wilmington whose origin is still obscure. The only other similar
human figure in Britain is the Cerne Abbas Giant in Dorset. Some
say the Long Man could be a Roman road engineer with his

'sighting posts' for fixing the direction but the latest theories are given on the plaque to be found on the Downs near the foot of the figure – you pass it on the Wealdway.

The Downs are a fine place for wild flowers and birds: in April the slopes above Wilmington are covered with cowslips and it is in the chalk that orchids are sometimes to be found (but never plucked). The skylark's song can be heard at all times of the year but probably the most common bird to be seen is the meadow pipit. The wheatear is another bird of the Downs: a summer visitor, it used to be snared with nets by the hundred to make wheatear pie. Thank goodness times are now less barbarous and you can often enjoy seeing this handsome bird flying in front of you. At migration times in spring and autumn flocks of birds of many kinds may be seen on their way in or out: I have seen dozens of whinchat resting on gorse bushes and a flock of goldcrest clinging to the cliff at Seaford Head in October. Yellowhammer and corn bunting are frequently to be seen and heard.

The gradients on this part of the Wealdway are gradual but long. After continuous rain parts of the path that are shared with horse-riders can be a quagmire but walkers should be able to find unofficial 'diversions' near the path to avoid the deep mud.

The Eight Bells inn at Jevington, right on the route, should be able to provide meals or bar snacks.

A 3½ mile diversion to Alfriston, one of Sussex's most attractive villages, is described on pages 214–217, with a sketch map.

MAPS
OS 1:50 000 199
OS 1:25 000 TQ 40/50, TV 49/59/69

Route southbound

From the carpark at the southern end of Wilmington's village street keep along the road and in about 300 m on the left is the bridleway climbing in the direction of the Long Man of Wilmington seen carved in the chalk 'looking naked towards the shires'. The path

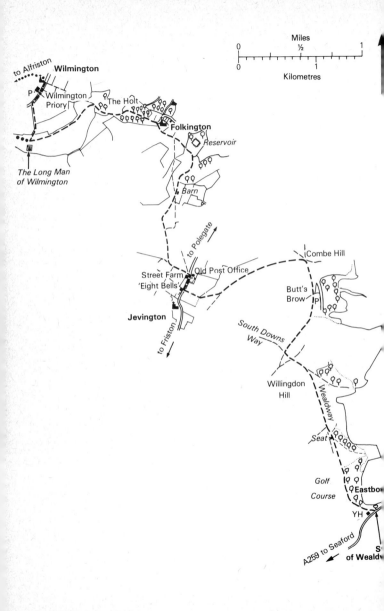

The Long Man of Wilmington looks down on the Wealdway

brings you to a descriptive plaque fixed below the figure; this gives the details and the various theories of its mysterious origin.

The Long Man is 73 m (237 ft) long and of unknown origin. No one knows whether it is Roman, Saxon, mediaeval or possibly pre-Roman. One would have thought it must be connected with the priory otherwise it would have been condemned as a heathen figure and left to become overgrown. Let us hope that some day more evidence will come to light.

From the plaque the Wealdway bears left along the track cut in the slope, dotted with cowslips in spring, continuing through a gate ('no motor cycles') and through the woods until you eventually come to the hamlet of Folkington.

Folkington is of Saxon origin and nowadays consists of the small flint and stone church right on the Wealdway, a farm and a Victorian manor house. The church was built in the thirteeenth century and the windows on each side of the chancel are of this period, as is the inside door of the porch. That the age was not without its violence is shown by a contemporary record that in 1271 a miscreant sought sanctuary in the church after having shot a man through the heart with an arrow and then fled the country.

The Wealdway continues by the track running to the right of the church, at first alongside a field and then starting to climb in a hollow, lined by bushes, until it crosses a 'saddle' between two heights in the Downs, passing a flint barn on the left before descending gradually. Turn left where the track meets another coming in from the right and you will soon come out on the road at Jevington, opposite the Old Post Office. Bear right along the road and you will reach the conveniently sited Eight Bells pub opposite which the next stretch of the Wealdway starts.

Jevington (Old English 'homestead of Geofa's people') is a very ancient downland settlement. Professor Margary has traced a Roman road from Polegate over the Downs to Jevington, branching off that from the fortress at Pevensey to the Lewes area. Between the Old Post Office and the Eight Bells you pass Street Farm. The word 'Street' or a variation of it often denotes a connection with a Roman road (examples are Streatham and Stratton on the Fosse) and it is likely that the name of the farm has a similar derivation. It is rewarding to walk down the road from the Eight Bells and take

Firle Beacon on the South Downs from the Long Man of Wilmington

the path on the right by the white railings to Jevington church, through a curious 'tapsell' gate. There is a charming setting and the church has one of the few Saxon towers in Sussex. Its massive construction, as mentioned in the descriptive booklet, suggests it played a defensive role against raiders. The date of the earliest parts of the building is given as about 950 AD. Flat Roman bricks have

Jevington from the slopes of Combe Hill

been incorporated in the construction, another sign of a Roman connection. The church represents every feature of English church architecture from the Saxon to the Perpendicular of the sixteenth century.

There is a restaurant farther down the road, The Hungry Monk, an old house said to have been a centre of smuggling, and beyond

The Hungry Monk is a carpark. On the way back to the Eight Bells, the house on the right, King's Farthing, formerly three cottages, is said to be connected by an underground passage to the inn, used for smuggling.

Opposite the Eight Bells there are steps and a waymarked post indicating the continuation of the Wealdway up the path on to the Downs. On reaching the stile the route bears left up the slope – quite a long climb. Keep to the grass path between the clumps of gorse – towards the top of the first rise there are two wooden posts to serve as a guide: pass between them. On the next rise there is a waymarked stile ahead. Keep straight on to the crest of the hill (Combe Hill 193 m – 630 ft).

As you reach the crest you may notice a ring of low banks in the form of a circle with another circle of low banks farther in, forming a ring 100 m in diameter across the crest. This is one of the few 'causewayed camps' in the south of Britain, said to be pastoral enclosures from Neolithic (New Stone Age) times (about 2500 BC) – the earliest 'civilised' inhabitants of Britain, having added to hunting the rearing of cattle, pigs and sheep and the growing of crops – a 'grain rubber' was found on Combe Hill – as means of livelihood. Instead of defence, the main purpose of these camps was more likely to have been to corral flocks and herds. The dating results from the finding of broken pottery. Inside the camp circle there are also tumuli or burial mounds from the Bronze Age (about 1500 BC).

From the top of Combe Hill you will see the white chalk cart-track curving away to the right and a carpark (Butts Brow) in the distance. You pass three concrete right-of-way signs on the left of the path. Make for the kissing-gate at the far right-hand boundary of the carpark. From this gate, turn right along the wide track and after about a mile you come to the trig point on the top of Willingdon Hill (201 m – 659 ft). There is a 'crossroad' of paths. Go past the trig point and in a few metres take the track on the left (there is a milestone with direction 'To Old Town'). This grass track

Combe Hill from the Wealdway

(with a cart-track beside it) gradually descends for almost a mile
before reaching a golf course. Pass behind the brick seat, a
memorial to a Methodist minister, and take the path in the 'corner'
seen in front of you. This is quite a wide track and runs for nearly
$\frac{3}{4}$ mile down to the main A259 Eastbourne–Brighton road, coming
out at the side of the youth hostel. The centre of Eastbourne, with

Eastbourne from East Dean Road near the southern start of the Wealdway

the railway station and bus terminus, is $1\frac{1}{2}$ miles down the A259 with the sea front another 800 m beyond. There is a request bus stop outside the hostel (half-hourly service weekdays; hourly Sundays).

Eastbourne is really an amalgamation of three small hamlets:

Bourne, Upperton and Seahouses. Bourne was the most important of these, with Seahouses a collection of fishermen's cottages and a few eighteenth-century lodging houses by the beach – one still survives, No. 6 Marine Parade. The passion for sea-bathing and the sea generally that started the huge growth of Brighton seems to have had little effect here, probably because the largest owners of the land, the Dukes of Devonshire, of Compton Place in the centre of Eastbourne – now a golf course – were not keen on a similar rapid development surrounding their pleasant acres. The 7th Duke however, noticing signs of the increasing popularity of the area, proceeded in the 1880s on extensive development using his enormous wealth to finance the building of avenues of opulent Victorian houses and amenities, creating an unusually well-planned community, welcomed by the better-off for holidays and residence. This development was helped by the opening in 1881 of a new railway line from London via Tonbridge (closed a few years ago) that shortened the route considerably. There had been a connection from Brighton via Lewes since 1849 but until this was electrified in the 1920s it had had little effect on Eastbourne's growth. The electrification plus the starting of light industry hastened the process, the population growing from 50,000 in 1921 to the present 70,000. The town has a good sunshine record and many attractions, including the 3 mile long promenade and easy access to the Downs and Beachy Head. An interesting connection with the Weald is Bel Tout, an old lighthouse on the cliff top above Beachy Head. This was built over 100 years ago by John Fuller of the famous iron-founder family of Heathfield, whose forefathers have on show in the Tower of London one of their eighteenth-century Sussex cannon stamped with the family initials 'JF'.

As you make your way down the hill from the end of the Wealdway you pass Old Town, the original 'Bourne', a Saxon village mentioned in the Domesday Book, with a sturdy Norman church and the old Lamb Inn next door. There are one or two old buildings built with flint and sometimes huge round stones from the beach – a real art.

The main Eastbourne Tourist Information Office is at 3 Cornfield Terrace (for accommodation information), and there is a smaller one in the shopping precinct at Terminus Road (this is near the railway station and bus terminus). There is also one in the summer months on the sea front: Lower Promenade, Grand Parade. They share the same telephone number, Eastbourne (0323) 27474, and have full information on accommodation and amenities.

Beachy Head above Eastbourne

Route northbound
The start of the Wealdway is on the A259 Eastbourne–Seaford–Brighton road 1½ miles from the centre of Eastbourne*, Terminus Road, where the railway station is situated and most of the bus services start. From here, if you are walking, follow the sign to the A259. It is quite a climb but of interest as you pass through Old

Town, with the Norman church, the Lamb Inn and old houses built
with flint. Walk on up the hill until you begin to leave the houses
behind and on the right you will see the youth hostel.

There is a bus from Terminus Road to the hostel (at the time of
writing it is the 712 with a half-hourly service on weekdays, hourly
on Sundays and holiday – ask to be put down at the youth hostel.
There is also the No 3 bus that goes within 800 m of the youth
hostel. Ask for East Dean Road, which is the address of the
hostel).

The Wealdway starts alongside the hostel, indicated by a
decorative and encouraging sign: 'Gravesend 80 miles'. For the first
800 m the route is along what seems to be a very old downland
track, used by foot-passengers and pack-horses over the years,
climbing gradually between thick bushes before eventually coming
out on a golf course by a brick-built seat, erected in memory of a
Methodist minister.

Turn right from behind the seat and follow the grass track for a
mile straight towards the crest of the high ground seen ahead,
ignoring the paths that branch off in various places. On the crest you
come to the trig point on Willingdon Hill (201 m – 659 ft). From the
trig point, take the track bearing sharply to the right (north-west).
At this 'crossroad' of paths there are two old milestone, one
indicating the route to Jevington. You do *not* take this one. 'Ours' is
the one with the indication 'Willingdon' although we do not go all
the way to Willingdon.

The Wealdway track curves, with a barbed wire fence on its left,
round to the left. Coming over the second rise in the path you
should be able to see the carpark of Butts Brow in front of you.

On reaching the carpark go through the kissing-gate and keep
straight on, on the cart-track showing white in the chalk, past three
concrete right-of-way signs to the right of the path. The track curves
round to the summit of the hill, Combe Hill* (193 m – 630 ft),
where there is the archaeologically important 'causewayed camp'.
Follow straight over the crest of Combe Hill and go through the stile
in the fence on the other side. From there the path descends over
the grass, keeping to the right of the slope. As you come over the
second rise in the ground from the stile you should see, on the right,

a stile at the start of a path that leads down to the road and the village of Jevington*, opposite the Eight Bells inn.

To continue from Jevington, turn right on the road (left, if you come out of the Eight Bells!). On the left, opposite the Old Post Office, there is a lane – the house Cooper's is on the corner. Turn up this lane and in about 400 m, on the right, it is joined by another track – there is a triangle of grass at the junction. Take this track on the right that climbs steadily until a flint barn by the side of the path is reached; from there the route descends between steep banks before emerging in about ¾ mile on more level ground near the old church at Folkington*.

From Folkington the right-of-way continues through the woods on the left (the 'Private' notice does not refer to walkers who keep to the path through the trees). At the far edge of the wood where the path forks take the left-hand path and go through the gate. From the gate the route curves round the slope of the Downs to the foot of that gigantic figure carved in the chalk, the Long Man of Wilmington*. There is a plaque describing the figure and the various theories concerning its origin.

Take the path to the right from the plaque, running northwards towards the road and the village of Wilmington* and its priory, seen to the right.

Diversion

Alfriston 3½ miles (an extra 3 miles)

Directions for southbound walkers
This diversion starts at the gate in the far (north-western) corner of the churchyard of Wilmington's ancient church. The path runs clearly over the fields, at first almost due west and then bearing half-left down the gentle slope on a grass track. While keeping in the same direction you cross two country roads – the stiles are practically opposite each other. At the third road, turn left opposite the farm, Milton Court Farm. The continuation of the path will be seen a short distance along the road in the hedge opposite the telephone kiosk.

You come out by a bridge over the Cuckmere River – there is a fine view of Alfriston and its church. Do not cross the bridge but cross the fence on the left, the path running along the river bank towards the church. Cross the river by the long white-painted footbridge, the White Bridge; carry straight on and this will bring you to Alfriston's main street with old inns, tea and antique shops, Post Office, etc. On the way to the main street you pass the green and the impressive church, the 'Cathedral of the Downs', and by its side, the unique Clergy House.

Alfriston (Old English 'Aelfric's homestead' – Aelfric is mentioned in the Domesday Book as one of the original landlords when the survey was made in 1086) is one of the most attractive and the most visited of Sussex villages. There has been a settlement of some importance on the site from just after the Romans left Britain in 450 AD In the early ears of this century a Saxon burial ground was found at Winston Street, the farm on the opposite side of the Cuckmere from Milton Court Farm, with over 150 graves and a treasure-house of Saxon bronze and silver work – some is to be seen in the Barbican Museum in Lewes. The great church was built in 1360: its cost must have been huge and evidence of the prosperity of the neighbourhood, not only of the local nobility, I should guess, but also of the people. Of intense interest is the old Clergy House on the south side of the church, in much the same form as when it was built in about 1350 of timbered frame with infilling of wattle and daub. It was in a state of ruin until in 1896 an energetic vicar persuaded the newly-formed National Trust to take it over – the very first building the Trust bought, at a cost of £10 (about £350 at present-day values) and £350 (£12,000) for the renovation. One amusing episode quoted in the Trust's descriptive booklet tells how when they renewed the floor of the house in 1977, following the original 'recipe' of rammed chalk sealed with sour milk, the new floor stank to high heaven for months afterwards! The booklet quotes more fascinating detail.

In the main street is the old Market Cross and the Star and other hostelries whose connections with smuggling were notorious. When the government of the day imposed taxes on commodities of one kind or another – in the case of the Sussex coast it was a tax on the

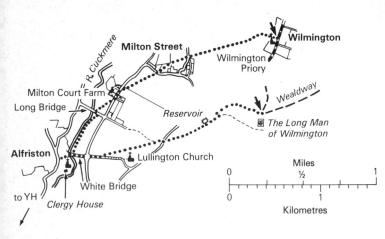

export of sheep-skins in the thirteenth-century – smuggling became a major industry: in the Middle Ages there was even a lively trade in Sussex cannon with friend or foe abroad, where the price fetched was much higher! You will find that most of the old inns and houses in Alfriston have some smuggling tale to tell.

The youth hostel is ¾ mile down the road southwards towards Seaford.

The rejoin the Wealdway retrace your steps across the White Bridge and keep straight on. Cross the road, the path continuing along the right-hand side of the barn. Some distance up the path there is a gate. Straight ahead, in about 500 m, is the tiny church of Lullington.

Lullington church is one of the smallest in Britain where services are still held. It is actually the chancel of the original thirteenth-century church. Many of the mediaeval features are preserved.

From the gate bear left for a few metres (or right if you are returning from Lullington church) for the path to Wilmington; the path runs diagonally half-left across the sloping hillside towards a stile in the field boundary. From there, it keeps in the same direction until another stile brings you to a sunken track. Turn right on this track, reaching the road a few metres ahead. Cross the road and take the wide track opposite, signed 'Jevington', through the gate, and up towards the crest of the rise. On the crest is a reservoir: turn off the track and make for the stile in the fence on the left. Go over this stile and ahead, a short way down the slope, is a metal 'spring' gate and a fenced track that continues round the hillside. This will bring you to the information plaque at the foot of the Long Man of Wilmington, rejoining the Wealdway.

Directions for northbound walkers
From the information plaque at the foot of the Long Man of Wilmington keep straight on along the 'terrace' track curving to the left round the slope. At the top of the rise go through the metal 'spring' gate and then bear left over the stile in the wire fence near the small reservoir. Go round the left-hand side of the reservoir, joining the wide track descending the slope to the road. Cross the road to the sunken track opposite. After a few metres there is a stile on the bank to the left of the track. Go over this stile, the path continuing diagonally half-right down the slope across the field. The spire of Alfriston church can be your guide: go across a stile and on to the bottom left-hand corner of the next field.

If you want to see the tiny Lullington Church* take the path branching off to the left by the gate for the 500 m to the site.

Through the gate near the corner of the field the path leads down to the road at the side of an old barn. Go straight over and then cross the long footbridge, the White Bridge, over the Cuckmere, bringing you to Alfriston church*, the old Clergy House* and the main street of Alfriston* itself.

To rejoin the Wealdway, return to the far side of the White Bridge, cross the stile immediately on the left and follow the path along the river bank. At the next bridge, go over the fence and the stile opposite, the path leading across the field to a road. Turn left on the road for a short distance, past the farm (Milton Court Farm) and over the stile on your right. From here the path keeps straight on, from stile to stile and over two country roads, for just over a mile eventually reaching the churchyard in Wilmington* and the Wealdway.

Public transport

Wilmington

Bus services Eastbourne–Polegate–*Wilmington*–Alfriston–Seaford: SD 126. Daily, two-hourly.

Jevington

Bus services Jevington–Polegate–Eastbourne: SD 193. Tuesday, Wednesday, Friday, a.m. Jevington–Eastbourne, noon Jevington–Polegate, noon Eastbourne–Jevington.

Eastbourne

British Rail Hourly fast services, daily. London–East Croydon–Lewes–Hastings–Brighton–etc. Local connections to coastal resorts.
Bus services Youth hostel (for start of Wealdway): SD 712. Weekdays, half-hourly; Sundays, hourly. Eastbourne–Seaford–Newhaven–Brighton: SD 712, as above. Horsebridge–Hellingly–Heathfield: SD 190/1. Weekdays, hourly, Sundays, two-hourly. Horsebridge–East Hoathly–Uckfield–E. Grinstead: SD 780. Weekdays only, approx. two-hourly. Polegate–Wilmington–Alfriston–Seaford: SD 126. Daily, two-hourly.

Note SD = Southdown. Service enquiries: telephone Brighton (0723) 606600.

Accommodation

Wilmington See Section 7.

Eastbourne
Youth Hostel   Members only.   At start of route.
East Dean Road
Eastbourne BN20 8ES
Telephone Eastbourne
(0323) 37294

Alfriston
Youth Hostel   Members only.
Frog Firle
Alfriston
Polegate
E. Sussex BN26 5TT
Telephone Alfriston
(0323) 870423

Bibliography

Wealdway Long-Distance Footpath, Wealdway Steering Group, 1981.

Wealdway: accommodation and transport, Wealdway Steering Group, 2nd edition, 1982.

Kent History, F.W. Jessup. Kent County Council, 1966.

The King's England: Kent, Arthur Mee. Hodder & Stoughton, 1969.

The King's England: Sussex, Arthur Mee. Hodder & Stoughton, 1964.

A History of Sussex, J.R. Armstrong. Darwen Finlayson, 1967.

The Sussex Landscape, Peter Brandon. Hodder & Stoughton, 1974.

Ashdown Forest, Garth Christian. Society of Friends of Ashdown Forest, 1967.

Wealden Iron, Ernest Straker. David & Charles, 1969.

Sussex, Esther Meynell, Robert Hale, 1947.

In Saxon Sussex, Alec Barr-Hamilton. Arundel Press, 1957.

Roman Ways in the Weald, I.D. Margary. Phoenix House, 1948.

An Archaeology of South-East England, Gordon J. Copley, Phoenix House, 1958.

Discovering Regional Archaeology: South Eastern England, Edward Sammes. Shire Publications, 1973.

Framed Buildings of the Weald, R.T. Mason. Coach Publishing House, 1964.

Concise Oxford Dictionary of English Place Names, E. Ekwall. Oxford University Press, 1974.

Victoria County Histories of Kent and Sussex

Dictionary of National Biography, Vol. XIV. Oxford University Press, 1964.

Buildings of England, edited by Nikolaus Pevsner:

West Kent and the Weald, John Newman. Penguin, 1976.

Sussex, Ian Nair. Penguin, 1973.

Many sources have been used in compiling this guide, including the works listed in the Bibliography which are recommended for further study. The Wealdway Steering Group's Guide is indispensable for the walker.

Many kind people have helped me in various ways but I would particularly like to mention the Public Libraries of Croydon, Tonbridge and Teynham; also Miss N.J. Swainson, Senior Library Assistant of Wye College, for providing me with information on Richard Harrys, pioneer fruit-grower of Henry VIII. Mr Brian Hoath of Fairwarp, expert and lecturer on Ashdown Forest, also gave me the benefit of his rich experience. Mr Tom Sawyer, who provided the photographs for this guide and who is a Kentish Man, gave me many ideas for which I am most grateful.

Index